Pitman New Era Shorthand

Anniversary Edition

Audrey O'Dea, Joan Sykes,
Julie Watson and Pamela Williams

PEARSON
Longman

Harlow, England • London • New York • Boston • San Francisco • Toronto
Sydney • Tokyo • Singapore • Hong Kong • Seoul • Taipei • New Delhi
Cape Town • Madrid • Mexico City • Amsterdam • Munich • Paris • Milan

Pitman New Era Shorthand

Pearson Education Limited
Edinburgh Gate
Harlow
Essex CM20 2JE
England

and Associated Companies throughout the world

Visit us on the World Wide Web at:
http://www.pearsoned.co.uk

First published 1988
Reprinted 1988, 1989, 1991, 1992, 1993, 1994, 1995, 1996, 1997 (twice), 1998 (twice),
          1999, 2002, 2003 (three times)

ISBN 0 582 29889 X

British Library Cataloguing-in-Publication Data
A catalogue record for this book is
available from the British Library.

Produced by Pearson Education Asia Pte Ltd
Printed in Singapore (B & JO)

Contents

Appendix III
Short forms

Appendix IV
Intersections

Appendix V
Key to theory check

Acknowledgements

The Authors and Publishers gratefully acknowledge the contribution made by Bryan Coombs to the writing of this book. They also wish to thank Bert Canning who so kindly read through the completed manuscript and commented upon it.

Study Plan

To help you with your studies, each unit of this book contains the following:

1 Theory examples

These should be drilled. Drilling is the writing of an outline many times until you are confident that you will never have any hesitancy in writing it. The first time you write an outline, write it carefully and get the feel of it, but at each repetition write faster and faster. As you write, say the word(s) to yourself. This is your own personal dictation system and is invaluable. It will help you to build up your vocabulary.

2 Reading and writing practice

Read each sentence several times, either by way of pre-dictation preparation, or as a remedial procedure in between each dictation. Reading is an easy way to develop your shorthand skill, which comes through instant recognition of each outline. Rapid reading develops rapid writing.

3 Short form and phrasing practice

Many common words and phrases have abbreviated outlines and you will meet a number of these in each of the units. It is essential that you learn these as you meet them in each unit. Familiarity in reading and writing these from dictation is a positive way to develop your speed. A full list of the short forms is given at the end of the book.

4 Practice dictation passages

These passages contain both the theory points and short forms learnt in the unit, and should be taken from live or recorded dictation. Try to repeat this dictation at least three times. This repetition is one of the key factors in speed building. After each dictation, read back from your shorthand notes; check the outlines and circle any errors; drill each correction and any outlines which caused hesitancy. Rapid-read the shorthand passage. Then take the repeat dictation. Correcting your errors will help you to progress.

5 Theory check

To test that you have understood the theory, each unit ends with a theory check. Write the shorthand for each word, or take it from dictation. You can check your outlines with those given in Appendix V.

Typewritten transcription

You should begin to type from your shorthand notes as soon as possible. Aim to produce mailable copy of all your shorthand notes, as you would do in a real business situation. When transcribing memorandums and letters, remember to display these correctly, as you would do in business or in an examination.

Additional study aids

Workbooks 1 and 2: Anniversary Edition
Facility Drills: Anniversary Edition

Once you have learnt the theory in the Anniversary Edition, there are many other Pitman New Era Shorthand books to help you add to your shorthand skills and to develop your speed.

Introduction

Shorthand is a way of rapidly writing spoken sounds and Pitman Shorthand provides a way of representing every sound heard in English words.

The system is phonetic; that is, words are generally written as they are sounded and not according to ordinary longhand spelling.

The English alphabet is made up of 26 letters — the vowels *a*, *e*, *i*, *o* and *u*, and the 21 consonants. The Pitman Shorthand alphabet has 24 consonants. With the exception of *W*, *Y* and *H*, the strokes representing these consonant sounds can be shown as the parts of a wheel:

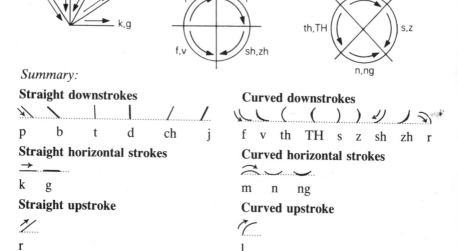

Summary:

Straight downstrokes

p   b   t   d   ch   j

Curved downstrokes

f   v   th   TH   s   z   sh   zh   r

Straight horizontal strokes

k   g

Curved horizontal strokes

m   n   ng

Straight upstroke

r

Curved upstroke

l

Specially formed upstrokes

w   y   h

Specially formed downstroke

h

Shorthand should be written as neatly and as accurately as possible. Although everyone has their own writing style, the size of the shorthand strokes in this book is a good standard to adopt in your own writing. The signs join easily with one another and they can be written with great speed when practised sufficiently. Write lightly and quickly, with only the slightest pressure to give the darker strokes.

Unit 1
Straight downstrokes

In Pitman Shorthand, the sounds heard in English words are divided into:

24 Consonants	12 Vowels	4 Diphthongs

and a shorthand sign is provided for each of these sounds.

The first six consonants are represented by light or darker straight strokes written downwards. Arrows indicate the direction in which strokes are written; they are never written in any other direction.

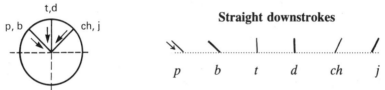

Never be tempted to sacrifice accurate formation of outlines for speed. You will find your speed naturally increasing with daily practice of writing neat and accurate outlines. Remember that your writing should always be as light as possible. All strokes are light but some strokes are lighter than others.

Letter	Sign	Phonetic name	As in		
P	⟍	pee	pay	tape	up
B	⟍	bee	be	rebate	curb
T	↓	tee	take	ate	it
D	↓	dee	day	edit	add
CH	⟋	chay	cheque	etch	which
J	⟋	jay	jet	edge	age

Note: These consonants form pairs; *P* and *B*, *T* and *D*, *CH* and *J*. In each pair a light sound is represented by a light stroke, and a corresponding heavy sound is represented by a darker stroke.

Position of outlines

Position writing is an important part of shorthand writing and vowel indication.

The outline is written:

1 above the line, in *first* position ⟍

2 touching the line, in *second* position ⟍

3 through the line, in *third* position ⟍

according to the *first vowel sound*.

In this unit and in Units 2 and 3 all the outlines are written in the second position.

This is the first of a number of exercises in this book to help you in your studies. Practise reading and writing these outlines:

Reading and writing practice — 1

As you read these outlines, say the sounds. Write the outlines from dictation.

1 ⟍⟍⟍ ⟍⟍ ⟍⟍⟍⟍⟍⟍   **4** ⟍⟍││//

2 ││ ││ ││││││   **5** │/⟍│/⟍

3 // // //////

Joining of consonants

Consonants are joined without lifting the pen, as in longhand. Begin the second where the first ends, and write each stroke in its proper direction. In this unit we are going to start writing in the second position, so the first stroke in each outline will rest on the line:

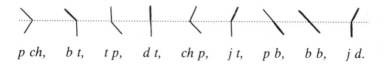

p ch,   b t,   t p,   d t,   ch p,   j t,   p b,   b b,   j d.

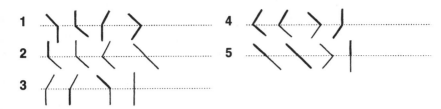

Vowels

Vowels are represented by dots and dashes written close to the consonant strokes. When a vowel comes *before* a consonant, it is placed *before* the stroke (left side) and when a vowel comes *after* a consonant, it is placed *after* the stroke (right side). Always write the consonant stroke first and then place the vowel sign.

The first upward or downward stroke takes the position of the first vowel sound in the word.

Vowels are written:

		Dots	Dashes
1	at the beginning of the stroke, in *first* place	⎸˙ ⎸˙	⎸‾ ⎸‾
2	in the middle of the stroke, in *second* place	⎸· ⎸·	⎸- ⎸-
3	at the end of the stroke, in *third* place	⎸. ⎸.	⎸_ ⎸_

Vowel a

The long vowel *a* is represented by a heavy dot and is written in second place:

pay,   paid,   page,   day,   date,   age,   ape,   babe,   bait.

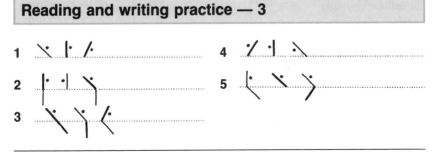

S circle

S circle is used to indicate the sound of *s* or *z* at the end of a word and is represented by a small circle written to the left (anti-clockwise):

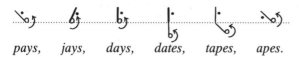

pays,   jays,   days,   dates,   tapes,   apes.

Reading and writing practice — 4

Vowel e

The short vowel *e* is represented by a light dot, and is a second-place vowel:

edge,   bet,   jet,   debt,   debts.

Reading and writing practice — 5

Short forms for common words

A few very frequently-used words, such as *it, to, but,* are expressed in shorthand by a single sign or abbreviated outline without vowels. Several are introduced in each unit and it is important to master them immediately by drilling them, as explained in the Study Plan at the beginning of this book. These short forms make up a considerable percentage of business and general dictation and they should be thoroughly memorized:

Short forms

⟍ be, ⎮ it, ⎮ do, ⁄ which, ⟍ to, ⟍ two/too, ⟍ but, ⟍ who, ⟍ the, ⟳ is/his, ⟩ object/objected.

S circle is also joined to short forms, eg ⟩ *objects*.

Phrasing

To help in rapid writing, shorthand words may often be joined. This is known as phrasing. Outlines should only be phrased when they join easily and naturally, the meaning being clear, as shown in the examples in this book. The first word in a phrase is written in its normal position:

Phrases

but which,   who is,   it is,   is it,   is to.

Some consonant strokes also represent phrases:

5⟍   20⟍

5 per cent,   20 per cent per annum.

Note: The sign for *per cent* must always be used with a figure, as shown, and not with a shorthand outline.

Tick the:
A small, light, slanting tick at the end of a word represents *the*. The tick is written either upwards or downwards, whichever forms the sharper angle:

pay the,   be the,   to the,   which the,   is the,   to do the,   is to.

Punctuation

The following special punctuation marks are used in shorthand:

capital letter, full stop, question, exclamation, hyphen, dash, brackets,

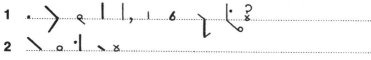

paragraph, stroke (oblique), underline or whole word in capital letters.
Other signs are written as in longhand.

Short form and phrasing practice

1

2

3

4

5

Practical dictation

1

2

3

4

5

6

7

8

9

10

11

12

13

14

15

Theory check

As a test of what you have learnt so far, write the following in shorthand:

1	which is	**6**	pep
2	pays the	**7**	page the
3	bays	**8**	babes
4	aid	**9**	do the
5	baits	**10**	date the

Unit 2
Curved strokes

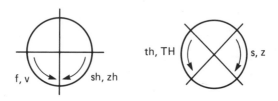

The next four pairs of consonants are all curves and are written downwards.

Letter	Sign	Name	As in		
F	↙	ef	face	laugh	file
V	↙	vee	video	shave	have
Th	⟨⟨	ith	thank	path	think
TH	⟨⟨	thee	then	bathe	this
S	⟩⟩	ess	sign	race	so
Z	⟩⟩	zee	zero	easy	was
Sh	⟋⟋	ish	she	cash	shall
Zh	⟋⟋	zhee	measure	leisure	usual

F, Th, S and *Sh* are light strokes and *V, TH, Z* and *ZH* are darker strokes:

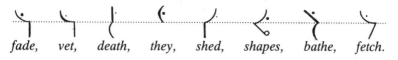

fade,   vet,   death,   they,   shed,   shapes,   bathe,   fetch.

The *stroke S* is used when *S* is the only consonant in a word, as in ...)⦁... *say*.

Stroke S is also used when a vowel is sounded before *S* at the beginning of a word and when a vowel follows *S* at the end of a word as in ...)... *ace*, ...)⦁... *say*, ...)⦁... *essay*.

Reading and writing practice — 1

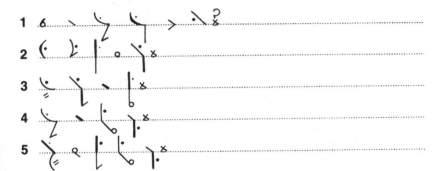

Vowels *o* and *u*

There are two more second-place vowels — the dash vowels.

1 Long *o* is represented by a heavy dash:

boat,   *vote*,   *photo*,   *oath*,   *bows*,   *sew/so*.

2 Short *u* is represented by a light dash:

up,   *us*,   *Dutch*,   *judge*,   *pup*.

Remember always to write the strokes of the outline first and then add the vowel sign.

Reading and writing practice — 2

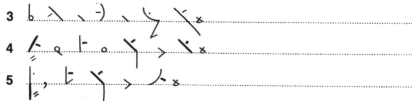

3

4

5

Short forms

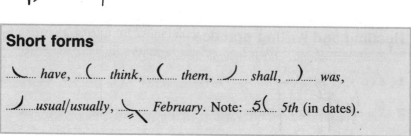

⟍ *have*, ⟨ *think*, ⟨ *them*, ⟋ *shall*, ⟩ *was*,
⟋ *usual/usually*, ⟍ *February*. Note: 5⟨ *5th* (in dates).

Note: As an aid to transcription, where a short form is a proper noun, the capital letter is indicated, as in *February*.

Short form and phrasing practice

Practical Dictation

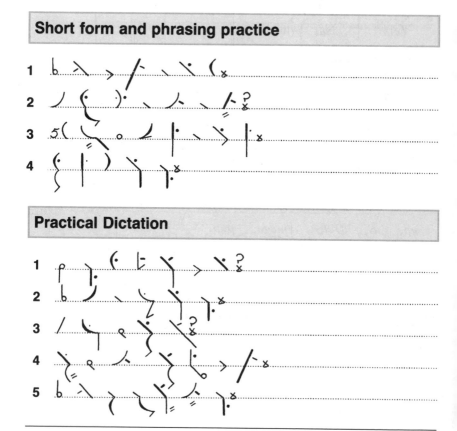

Theory check

Write the following in shorthand:

1	shape	6	depot
2	essay	7	edge
3	jet	8	show
4	thud	9	fed
5	fade	10	votes

Unit 3
Horizontal strokes; upward strokes

The next consonants are all written forward (from left to right) and are light strokes, except for *G* and *NG*:

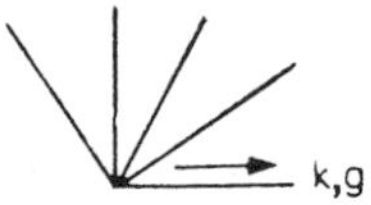

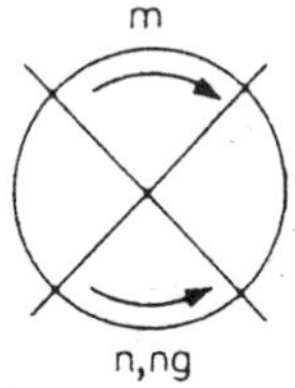

Letter	Sign	Name	As in		
K		kay	company	luck	kind
G		gay	gain	give	big
M		em	may	seem	him
N		en	no	know	seen
NG		ing	long	bank	thing

When a vowel comes *before* a horizontal stroke it is written *above* the stroke; when a vowel comes *after* a horizontal stroke it is written *below* the stroke:

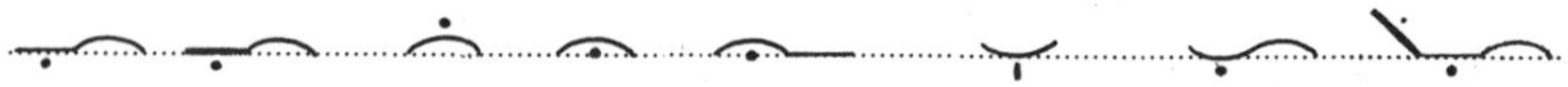

came, *game*, *aim*, *may*, *make*, *no/know*, *name*, *became*.

Reading and writing practice — 1

1 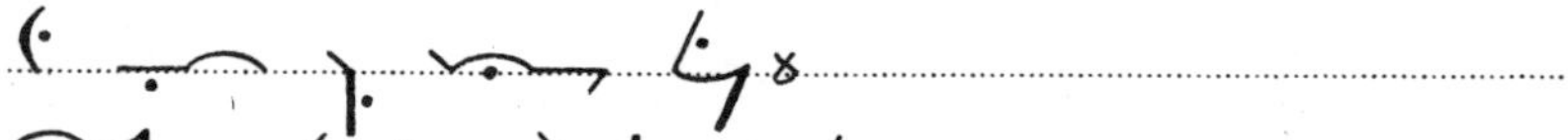

2 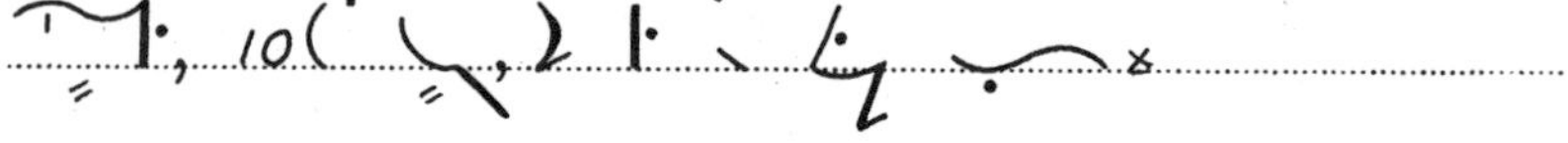

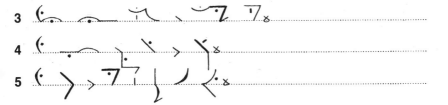

Upward strokes

The following consonants are written upwards and are light strokes:

Letter	Sign	Name	As in		
L	↗	el	lie	mail	will
W	↙	way	weigh	we	aware
Y	↙	yay	youth	yes	yellow

Vowels to upstrokes are placed to the *left* when they come before a consonant and to the *right* when they follow a consonant:

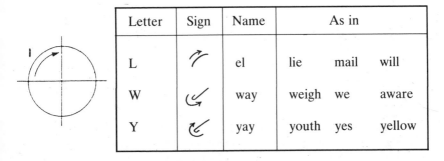

length, load, mail, coal, delayed, way/weigh, wage, yellow, yes.

Reading and writing practice — 2

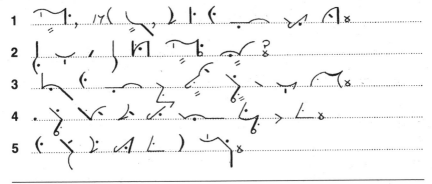

Short forms

.... *come*, ... *give/given*, ... *him*, ... *thing*, ... *we*,

.... *never*, ... *inform / informed*, ... *January*, ... *November*.

Phrases

In a phrase, after a downstroke, the stroke *l* represents the word *will*:

it will,   *which will*,   *who will*,   *they will be*,   *it will have*.

Intersections

   A single stroke may represent a complete word when written through or written close to another outline. It is a useful device to represent common words and may be adapted to special vocabulary needs. It is helpful if intersections through words of joined consonants are written through the first stroke, if the intersection is read first, or through the final stroke if the intersection is read second.

Intersected *K* represents *company*:

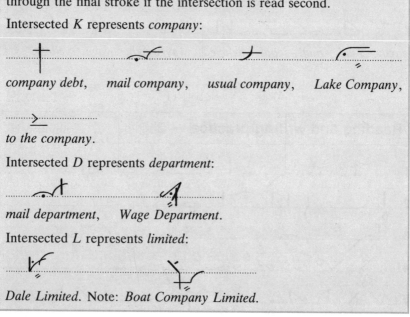

company debt,   *mail company*,   *usual company*,   *Lake Company*,

to the company.

Intersected *D* represents *department*:

mail department,   *Wage Department*.

Intersected *L* represents *limited*:

Dale Limited. Note: *Boat Company Limited*.

Short form and phrasing practice

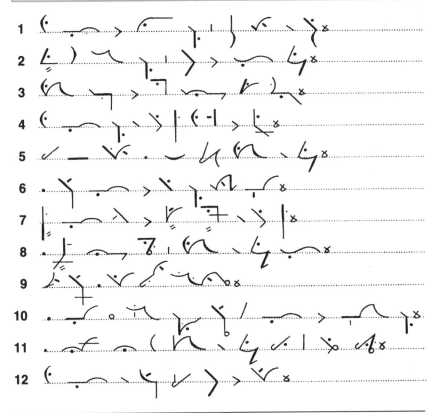

Practical dictation

13 [shorthand outline]

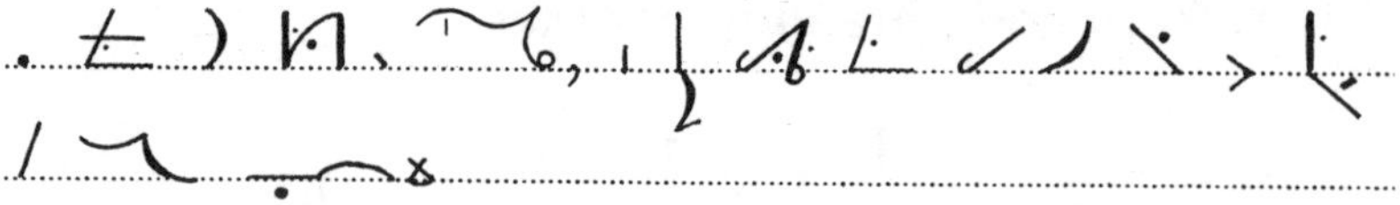

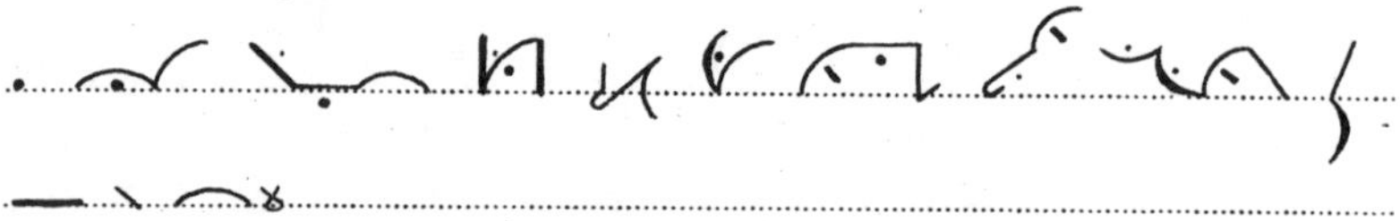

14 [shorthand outline]

15 [shorthand outline]

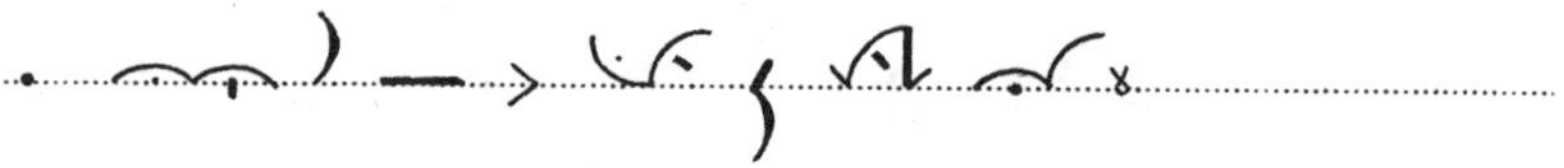

Theory check

Write the following in shorthand:

1	make	**6**	yoke
2	length	**7**	wedge
3	escapes	**8**	wage department
4	joke	**9**	envelope
5	vague	**10**	it will be

Unit 4

First-place vowels

When the first vowel in a word is a first-place vowel:

1 the outline is written in first position, with the first upstroke, downstroke or horizontal stroke above the line;
2 the vowel is placed at the beginning of the stroke;
3 where the first stroke is a horizontal, followed by an upstroke or downstroke, it is the upstroke or downstroke which takes the position.

There are four first-place vowels.

Two dot vowels:

1 Long *ah* — represented by a heavy dot

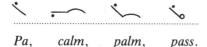

Pa,   calm,   palm,   pass.

2 Short *a* — represented by a light dot

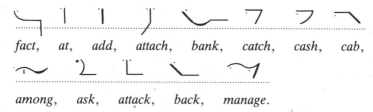

fact,   at,   add,   attach,   bank,   catch,   cash,   cab,

among,   ask,   attack,   back,   manage.

Reading and writing practice — 1

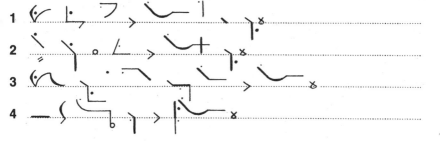

5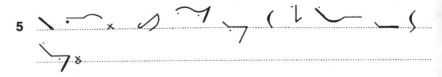

Two dash vowels:

1 Long *aw* — represented by a heavy dash

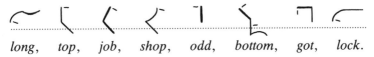

saw, bought, auto, law, talk.

Note: Before the upstroke *L*, the *aw* vowel may be joined, eg 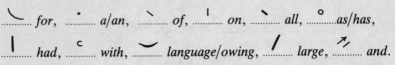 *also.*

2 Short *o* — represented by a light dash

long, top, job, shop, odd, bottom, got, lock.

Reading and writing practice — 2

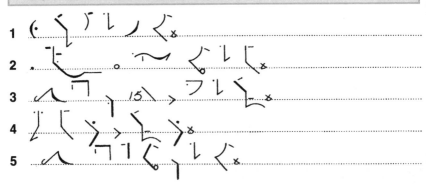

Short forms

⌣ *for,* · *a/an,* ＼ *of,* | *on,* ＼ *all,* ° *as/has,*

| *had,* ᶜ *with,* ⌣ *language/owing,* / *large,* ⁊ *and.*

Short form and phrasing practice

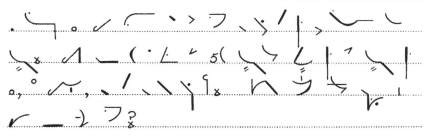

Practical dictation

1 Telephone instructions dictated to secretary by Area Sales Manager

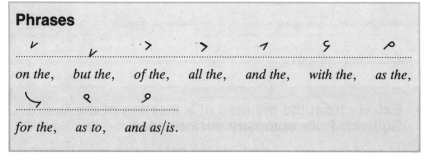

2 Memo to: Shop Manager   From: Security Chief
Subject: Anticipated robbery   Date: Today's

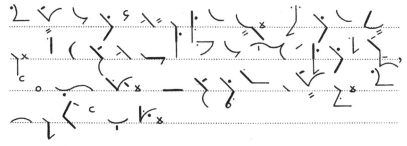

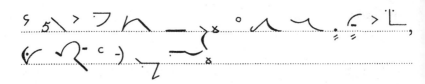

3 Extract from the minutes of a meeting of the Board
Subject: Poor company performance

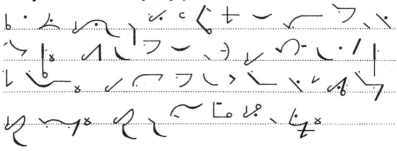

Write the following in shorthand:

1	at	6	manage
2	calm	7	off
3	tall	8	damage
4	away	9	talk
5	got	10	knock

Unit 5
Third-place vowels

The last four vowels are written in the third place. This means that:

1 the outline is written with the first upstroke or downstroke through the line;
2 the vowel is placed at the end of the stroke;
3 when a vowel comes between two strokes, it is put in third place before the *second* stroke.

There are four third-place vowels.

Two dot vowels:

1 Long *e* — represented by a heavy dot

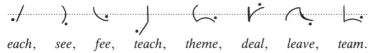

each,   see,   fee,   teach,   theme,   deal,   leave,   team.

2 Short *i* — represented by a light dot

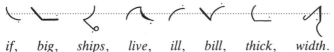

if,   big,   ships,   live,   ill,   bill,   thick,   width.

The short *i* is also used to represent the sound of *y* at the end of a word

money,   copy,   monthly,   apology,   many,   daily,   lady.

Reading and writing practice — 1

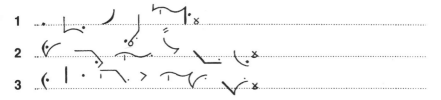

4

5

Two dash vowels:

1 Long *oo* — represented by a heavy dash

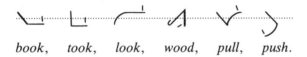

chew, shoe, food, pool, youth, tool, move.

2 Short *oo* — represented by a light dash

book, took, look, wood, pull, push.

Reading and writing practice — 2

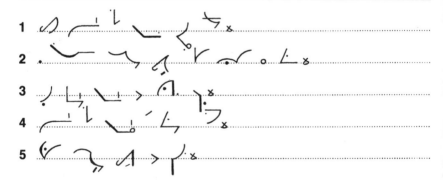

1

2

3

4

5

Third-place horizontal outlines

1 When the first vowel is a third-place vowel and the outline consists only of horizontal strokes, the outline is written on the line

key, cook, ink.

2 When the outline begins with a horizontal stroke, followed by an upstroke or downstroke, the upstroke or downstroke is written in the third place

keep,   move,   meal.

Note: -ing ending is written leaving out the *i* vowel

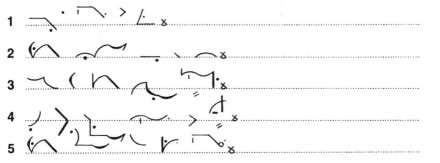

making,   taking,   living,   looking,   asking,   mailing.

Reading and writing practice — 3

1

2

3

4

5

Short forms

...) wish, ...\... put, ...\... to be, ...|... different/difference, ...'↓... owe,

... can, ... go, ...'↓... ought, ... in/any, ... young,

... anything, ... nothing.

Phrases

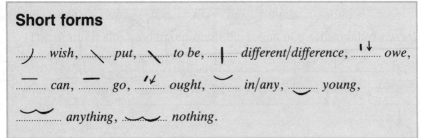

we wish,   in the,   to be the,   ought to be,   to go (vowel is inserted to distinguish from *to give*).

Intersections

P represents *party*: ....✗.... *big party*

   or *policy*: ....✗.... *bank policy*

B represents *bank*: ....✗.... *at the bank*

Short form and phrasing practice

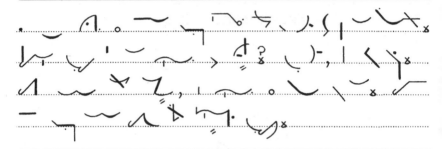

Practical dictation

1 Confidential memo from Company Secretary to Managing Director

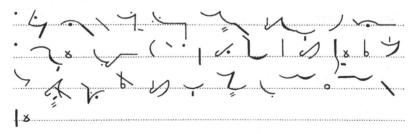

2 Memo from Chief Cashier to a new member of the department

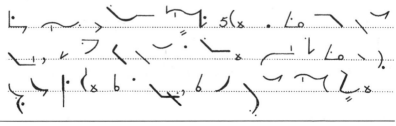

3 Note from Export Manager to his secretary

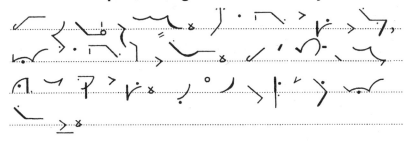

Write the following in shorthand:

1 ease
2 cool
3 leaving
4 keeps
5 feed

6 inch
7 king
8 talking
9 lucky
10 family

Summary of vowels

There are six long vowels, represented by a heavy dot or dash and six light vowels, represented by a light dot or dash.

These *mnemonic* sentences use all the vowel sounds, in order according to their positions:

Pa may we
All go too

That pen is
Not much good

They will help you to remember your vowels:

	Vowels	1st place	2nd place	3rd place
heavy {	•	*Pa*	*may*	*we*
	–	*All*	*go*	*too*
light {	•	*That*	*pen*	*is*
	–	*Not*	*much*	*good*

Unit 6

S circle; downward *L*

The consonants *S* and *Z* are two of the most important of all the consonants because they occur so frequently. They are represented by a small circle ⟨°⟩ as well as by the strokes ⟨⟩ *S* and ⟨⟩ *Z*, all of which you have already met.

The small circle joins easily to other consonant strokes at the beginning, in the middle or at the end of an outline. At the beginning of an outline the *S* circle is read first; at the end of an outline it is read last.

S circle

1   *S* circle is written inside a curve

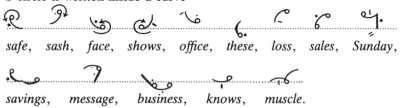

safe,   sash,   face,   shows,   office,   these,   loss,   sales,   Sunday,

savings,   message,   business,   knows,   muscle.

Reading and writing practice — 1

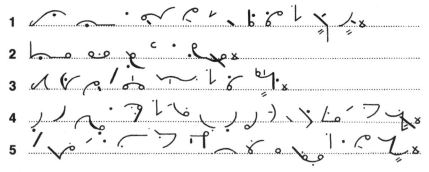

2   *S* circle is written with a left (anti-clockwise) motion to straight strokes, that is on the right-hand side of straight downstrokes and on the upper

side of straight horizontal strokes and straight upstrokes

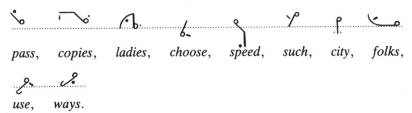

pass,   copies,   ladies,   choose,   speed,   such,   city,   folks,

use,   ways.

3 *S* circle is written on the outside of the angle formed by two straight strokes

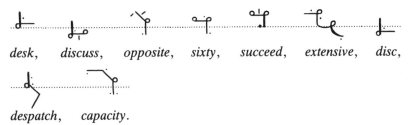

desk,   discuss,   opposite,   sixty,   succeed,   extensive,   disc,

despatch,   capacity.

Reading and writing practice — 2

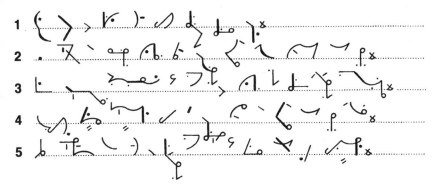

1

2

3

4

5

Strokes S and Z

1 In words beginning with *Z* the stroke *Z* ⟩ is used

⟩ *zoo,* ⟩ *zeal,* ⟩ *zinc.*

2 When a word begins with a vowel followed by the sound of *S/Z*, stroke *S/Z* must be written in order to place the initial vowel sign

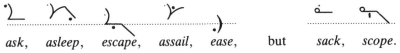

ask,   asleep,   escape,   assail,   ease,   but   sack,   scope.

3 When S/Z + vowel ends a word, the stroke S ⌣ or Z ⌣ is used

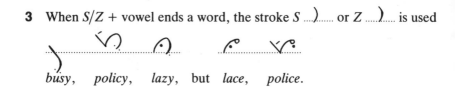

busy, policy, lazy, but *lace, police.*

The use of the stroke S/Z or S circle therefore indicates the presence or absence of a vowel at the beginning and end of outlines, and it is not necessary to place vowels in outlines using stroke S/Z.

Reading and writing practice — 3

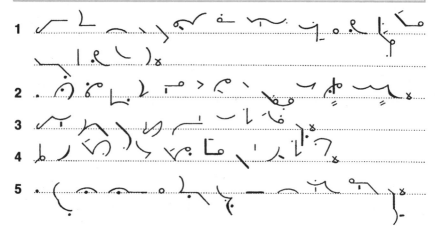

Downward L

Although L is usually written upwards 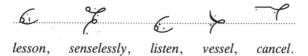, sometimes it is easier to write it *downwards* :

1 when stroke L precedes or follows S circle attached to a curve, it is written in the same direction as the circle:

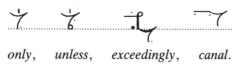

lesson, senselessly, listen, vessel, cancel.

2 after N or NG:

only, unless, exceedingly, canal.

Reading and writing practice — 4

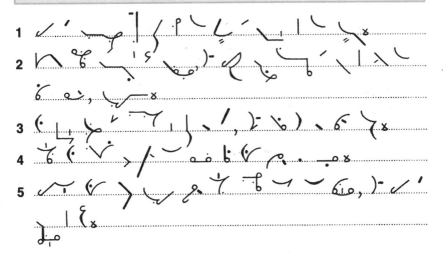

3 When a word begins with a vowel which is followed by *L* and a simple horizontal stroke write downward *L*

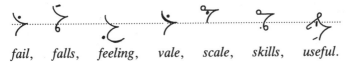

along, elm, alone,   but   *long, lame, look.*

4 When L follows ‿ *F,* ‿ *V* and �""⌐ *SK* or a straight upstroke, and a vowel does not end the word write downward *L*

fail, falls, feeling, vale, scale, skills, useful.

Special outlines:

column, film.

Note: As has already been seen, when a vowel ends the word, *L* is usually written upwards:

fully, awfully, yellow.

Reading and writing practice — 5

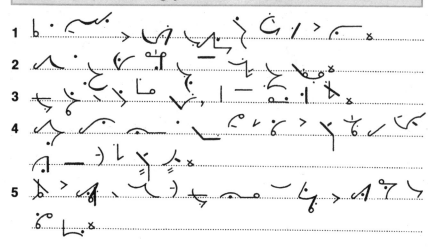

Remember that the *S* circle can be added to short forms:

objects, thinks, comes, gives, things, informs, languages,

wishes.

Phrases

1 *much*:

as much as,   as much as possible,   as much as it is.

but for easy joining

so much,   too much.

2 *us* — final *S* circle represents the word *us* in such phrases as:

for us,   to us,   give us,   take us,   show us,   making us,   with us.

3 Other phrases:

because of the,   for this,   for those (note distinguishing vowel),

for sale,   this will,   in some,   for some,   large sums.

Intersections

G represents *government*:   Japanese government

   this government

F represents *form*:   customs form

   in the form

Bs represents *business*:   law business

   big business

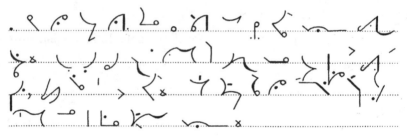

1 Memo regarding an enquiry for special lace

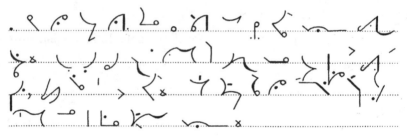

2 Report about an order from a business agency

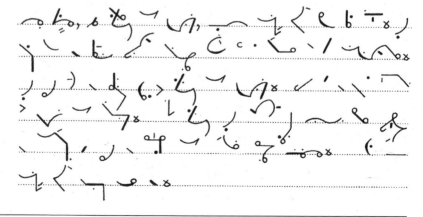

3 Memo to Despatch Department

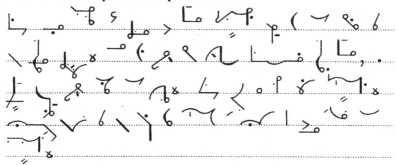

Write the following in shorthand:

1 looks
2 envelopes
3 justice
4 safely
5 succeeds

6 falling
7 vale
8 valley
9 skills
10 speaks

There are two forms for *R*, both written lightly in the direction of the arrows:

Letter	Sign	Name	As in		
R	⟋	ray	right	wrote	carry
	⤸	ar	air	early	car

R has two forms to make the joining of strokes easier, and also to indicate an initial or final vowel sound.

Downward *R* is written:

1 initially when preceded by a vowel

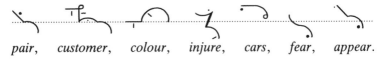

air, or, ear, ore, early, erase, oral.

2 finally when the sound of *R* ends a word

pair, customer, colour, injure, cars, fear, appear.

Note: Words which end in *-ore* or *-air*, however spelled, are written with a heavy second-place vowel:

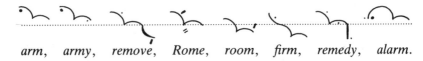

oar, door, shore, four, fair, share, spare, pear.

3 before *M* for ease of joining

arm, army, remove, Rome, room, firm, remedy, alarm.

Reading and writing practice — 1

Upward *R* is written:

1 when a word begins with the sound of *R*

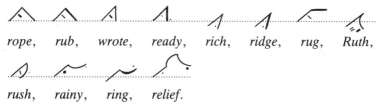

rope, rub, wrote, ready, rich, ridge, rug, Ruth,

rush, rainy, ring, relief.

2 finally when a word ends *R*-vowel

borrow, factory, injury, carry, sorry, varies, thorough.

Reading and writing practice — 2

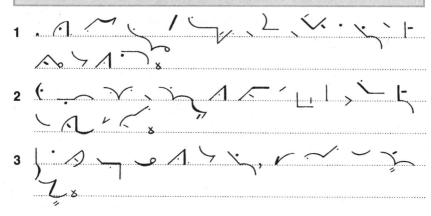

4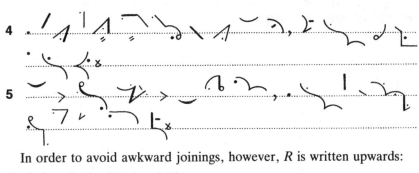

5

In order to avoid awkward joinings, however, *R* is written upwards:

1 *before* T, D, CH, J *and* Th

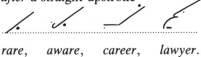

erratic,   arid,   arch,   urge,   earth.

2 *after* a straight upstroke

rare,   aware,   career,   lawyer.

3 *usually* in the middle of a word

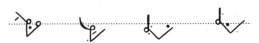

March,   party,   park,   authority,   garage,   charge.

4 *after* 2 downstrokes

upstairs,   visitor,   disappear,   despair.

Note: After 2 upstrokes, downward *R* is written, eg ⟋⟍ *rarer.*

5 *following* left motion curves and *S* circle, and *KS/GS*

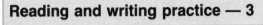

officer,   answer,   sincere,   boxer,   geyser.

Reading and writing practice — 3

1

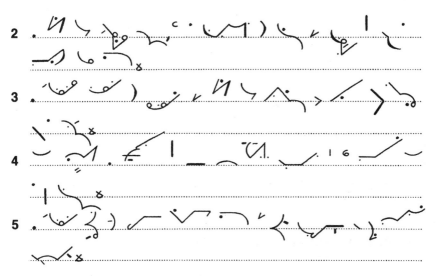

2 ...

3 ...

4 ...

5 ...

Short forms

..*.. are, ..*.. our/hour, ..*.. should, ...⌐... your, ...⌐... year,
(.... thank/thanked, ..ɔ.. what, ..ƒ.. satisfactory.

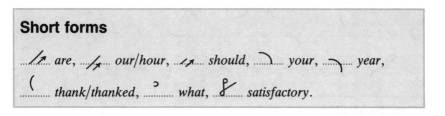

Phrases

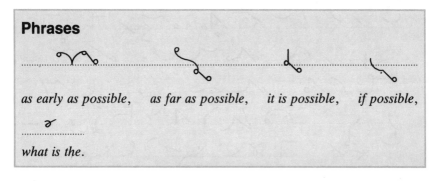

as early as possible, *as far as possible,* *it is possible,* *if possible,*

what is the.

Short form and phrasing practice

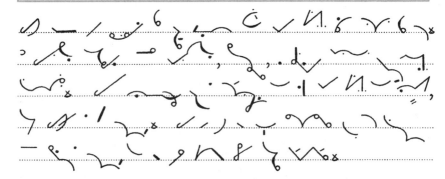

Practical dictation

1 Footwear shop seasonal sale

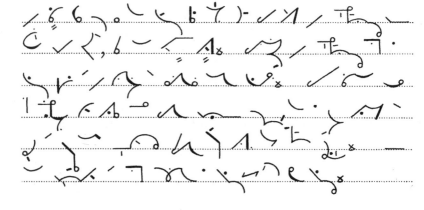

2 Memo to: Site Foreman   From: Works Manager
Subject: Removal of refuse   Date: Today's

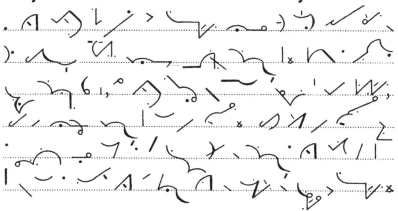

3 Car servicing advertisement

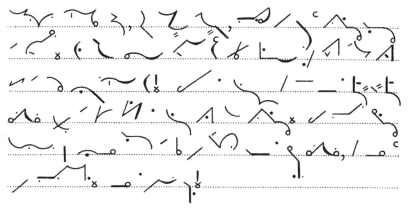

Write the following in shorthand:

1	charge	6	deter
2	repair	7	beware
3	salary	8	arrears
4	cashier	9	censor
5	erratic	10	we shall arrange

Unit 8
Diphthongs, triphones and diphones

Diphthongs

There are four diphthongs:

I, OI, OW, and *U*, as heard in the words 'I enjoy loud music'.

There are two first-place diphthongs:

1 *I* — represented by ‿‿‿‿

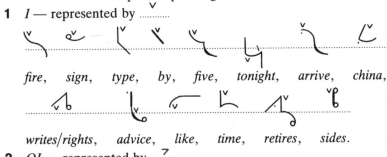

fire,   sign,   type,   by,   five,   tonight,   arrive,   china,

writes/rights,   advice,   like,   time,   retires,   sides.

2 *OI* — represented by ‿‿‿‿

boy,   toy,   annoy,   enjoy,   invoice.

Reading and writing practice — 1

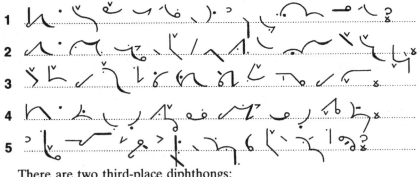

1

2

3

4

5

There are two third-place diphthongs:

1 *OW* — represented by ‿‿∧‿‿

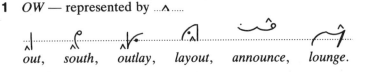

out,   south,   outlay,   layout,   announce,   lounge.

2 *U* — represented by

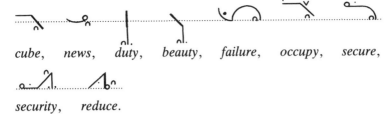

cube,   news,   duty,   beauty,   failure,   occupy,   secure,

security,   reduce.

Special outline: 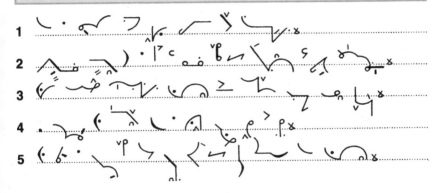 *volume.*

Note: Distinctive outlines 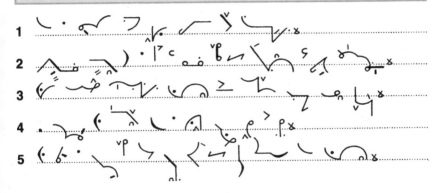 *pure,* 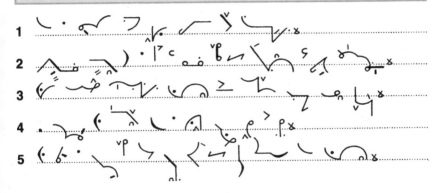 *poor.*

Reading and writing practice — 2

1 ....

2 ....

3 ....

4 ....

5 ....

Joined diphthongs

The diphthong signs are joined to strokes when an easy joining can be made:

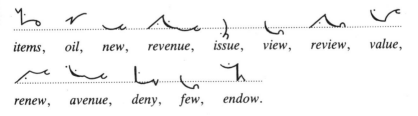

items,   oil,   new,   revenue,   issue,   view,   review,   value,

renew,   avenue,   deny,   few,   endow.

Note: *now*   because of the shape of the *OW* diphthong, the first part of the symbol is incorporated into the *N* stroke.

Reading and writing practice — 3

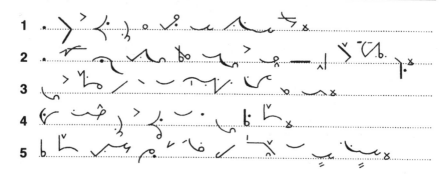

1
2
3
4
5

Triphones

A small tick added to the diphthong sign indicates another vowel following the diphthong:

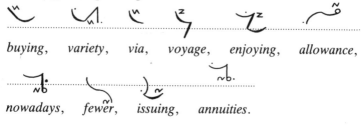

buying,   variety,   via,   voyage,   enjoying,   allowance,

nowadays,   fewer,   issuing,   annuities.

Reading and writing practice — 4

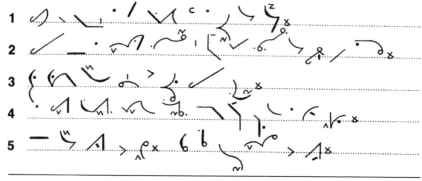

1
2
3
4
5

Triphones and stroke *S*

Stroke *S* is written:

1 in words where a triphone immediately follows initial *S*

science,   sighing,   suing,   suicide,   sewer.

2 in words where the final syllable *-ous* is immediately preceded by a diphthong

tenuous,   fatuous,   joyous.

Reading and writing practice — 5

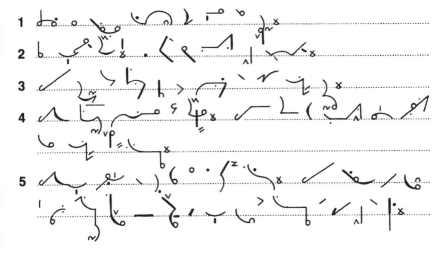

Diphones

Two consecutive vowels, pronounced as two separate syllables

(eg *copier*), are represented by ⌄ and ⌐ which are the diphone signs.

The sign is written in the place of the first vowel of the combination.

1  .... represents a dot vowel followed by one other vowel:

copier, senior, idea, theory, area, obvious, audio, serious,

really, video.

2 .... represents a dash vowel followed by one other vowel:

following, showing, ruinous, knowing, lower.

Reading and writing practice — 6

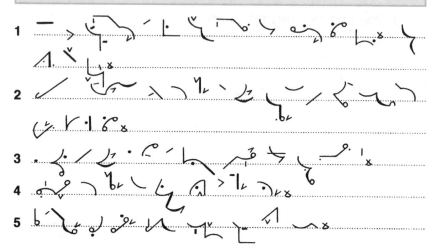

Phrases

1   Because of the shape of the *I* diphthong, the second part of the symbol is incorporated in strokes *L*, *M*, *K*, and upward *R* to form such phrases as:

I will,   I am,   I may,   I can,   I write.

2   The short form *you* is turned on its side to form

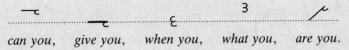

can you,   give you,   when you,   what you,   are you.

3   Other phrases:

9 am,   2 pm,   to me,   to him (note vowel).

Intersections

T represents *attention*: ......⌐ *for your attention.*

CH represents *charge*: ....✗.... *this charge.*

Short form and phrasing practice

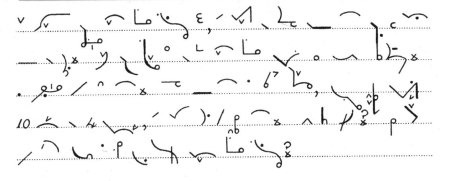

1 Letter to travellers about surcharge on holiday

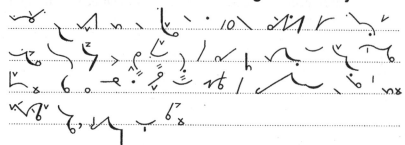

2 Extract from a financial report on share speculation

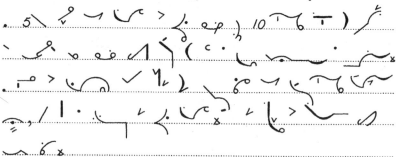

3 Memo to: Security Officer   From: Construction Manager
Subject: Investigation into   Date: Today's
site accident

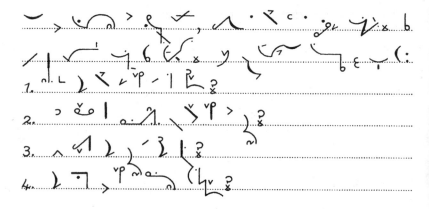

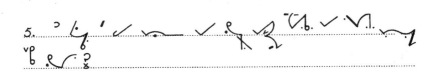

5. ....

Theory check

Write the following in shorthand:

1 knife
2 copier
3 bureau
4 tenuously
5 power

6 various
7 loyal
8 county
9 eyes
10 earlier

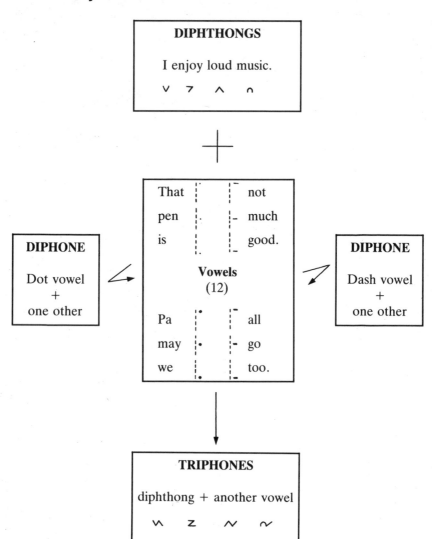

Unit 9
Consonant H

There are four ways of writing the consonant *H*:

Letter	Sign	Name	As in
H	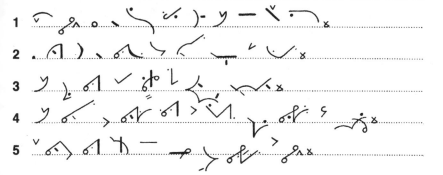	Upward ↗ Hay	hope hang house head
H		Downward ↙ Hay	he high hake hoax
H		Tick H	home hall hair
H	.	Dot H	mishap leasehold

Upward *HAY* is a light upstroke and is the most commonly used form:

hope,   hotel,   house,   head,   heavy.

Reading and writing practice — 1

1

2

3

4

5

Downward *HAY* 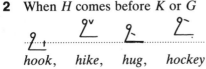 is a light downstroke and is only used:

1 When *H* is the only consonant sound in a word, and in the derivatives of such words

high,   higher,   highly,   hoe,   he.

2 When *H* comes before *K* or *G*

hook,   hike,   hug,   hockey.

3 When it is easier to write in the middle of a word

anyhow.

Reading and writing practice — 2

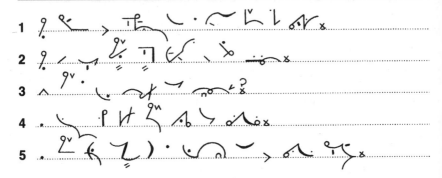

1

2

3

4

5

Tick H — A small tick sloping from right to left represents *H* before *M*, *L* and Downward *R* at the beginning of a word

home,   whole,   help,   hear/here.

Note: The word *HoMeLieR* will help you to remember when to use *Tick H*.

The angle of *Tick H* is very important to avoid confusion with the short form *to* .... or *but* .....

Reading and writing practice — 3

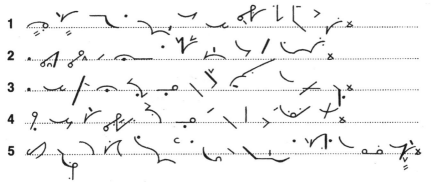

Dot H — In a few cases, where it would be difficult to write the stroke *H* in the middle of a word, *H* may be expressed by a light dot. This dot is placed alongside the vowel sign:

mishap,   likelihood,   household,   uphill,   unhappy.

Reading and writing practice — 4

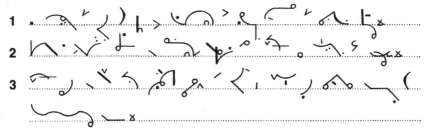

Short forms

manufacture/manufactured,   *manufacturer,*

would,   *whose,*   *he.*

Phrases

1 The short form for *he* 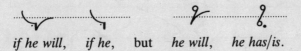 can only be used in the *middle* or at the *end* of a phrase, otherwise downward *H* is used:

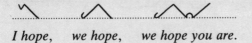

if he will, *if he,* but *he will,* *he has/is.*

2 When the word *hope* follows *I* or *we*, it is represented only by the stroke *P*:

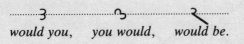

I hope, *we hope,* *we hope you are.*

3 *Would*:

would you, *you would,* *would be.*

Intersections

Stroke *S* represents *society*: .... *this society,* .... *our society.*

Short form and phrasing practice

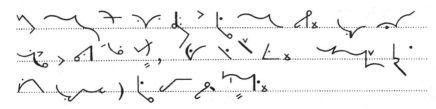

1 Letter to a publisher

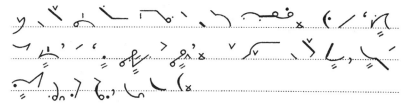

2 Memo to sales representative from Sales Manager

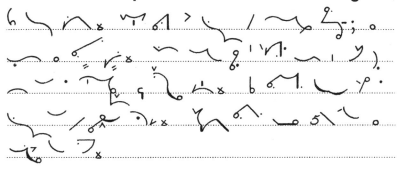

3 Letter to a local estate agent

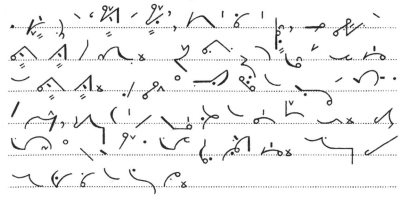

Write the following in shorthand:

1 heavy
2 heading
3 hang
4 hoax
5 hectic

6 mahogany
7 harm
8 help
9 whom
10 livelihood

Unit 10
ST, STR, SES and SWAY

ST Loop

A shallow loop, written in the same direction as the *S* circle, represents *ST* (called '*STEE*') and is half the length of the stroke to which it is attached. It is written:

1 At the beginning and end of curves

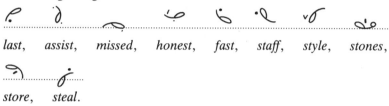

last, assist, missed, honest, fast, staff, style, stones,

store, steal.

2 At the beginning and end of straight strokes

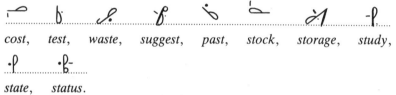

cost, test, waste, suggest, past, stock, storage, study,

state, status.

3 In the middle of some words

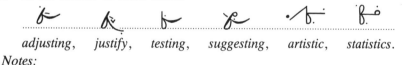

adjusting, justify, testing, suggesting, artistic, statistics.

Notes:

a The addition of *S* circle:

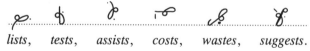

lists, tests, assists, costs, wastes, suggests.

b The *STEE* loop can represent a heavy final sound also:

used, paused, supposed, itemised, advised.

c When a vowel occurs between *S* and *T*, the *STEE* loop is not used:

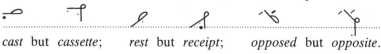

cast but *cassette; rest* but *receipt; opposed* but *opposite.*

d When a vowel ends a word, the stroke *T* must be written in order to place the vowel sign:

honest but *honesty*;   *modest* but *modesty*;   *haste* but *hasty*.

e Distinctive outlines: .... *cost*, ... *caused*.

Reading and writing practice — 1

1 ....

2 ....

3 ....

4 ....

5 ....

STR Loop

A large final loop written in the same direction as the *S* circle, extending two-thirds of the length of the stroke to which it is attached, represents *STER*:

poster,   administer,   investor,   master,   faster,   register.

Note: The addition of *S* circle:

posters,   investors,   masters,   registers.

Reading and writing practice — 2

1 ....

2 ....

3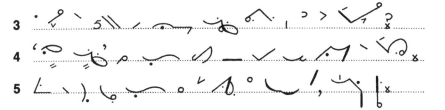

4

5

SES Circle

A large circle written in the same direction as *S* circle represents *SES*, *ZES* or *SEZ*:

1 at the end of words

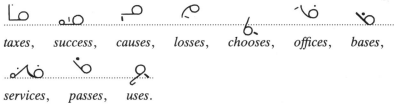

taxes,   success,   causes,   losses,   chooses,   offices,   bases,

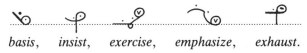

services,   passes,   uses.

2 in the middle of some words

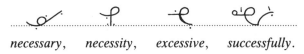

necessary,   necessity,   excessive,   successfully.

Notes:

a Any vowel other than the short *e* between the two *s*'s is indicated by writing the vowel sign inside the circle:

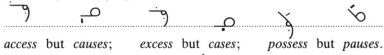

basis,   insist,   exercise,   emphasize,   exhaust.

b A few words ending in *s-s* are written with the *S* circle and stroke *S* for distinguishing purposes:

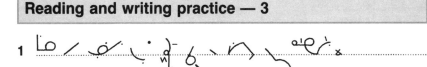

access but *causes;   excess* but *cases;   possess* but *pauses.*

c Downward *L* is written in: *necessarily.*

Reading and writing practice — 3

1

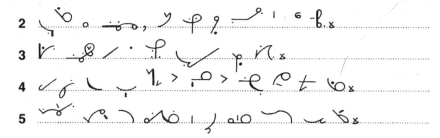

SW Circle

A large initial circle written in the same direction as the *S* circle represents *SW* (called '*SWAY*')

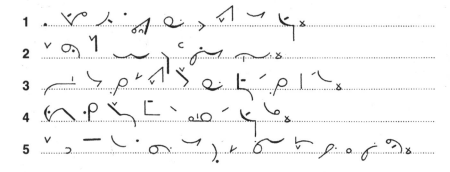

swing,   switch,   swelling,   swear,   swim,   swayed.

Reading and writing practice — 4

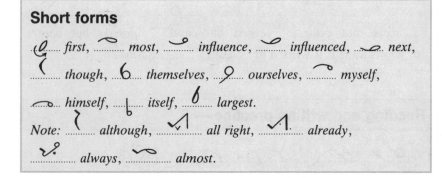

Short forms

first, *most*, *influence*, *influenced*, *next*, *though*, *themselves*, *ourselves*, *myself*, *himself*, *itself*, *largest*.

Note: *although*, *all right*, *already*, *always*, *almost*.

Phrases

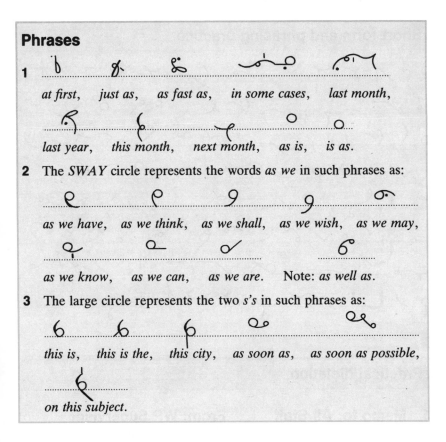

1 at first, just as, as fast as, in some cases, last month,

last year, this month, next month, as is, is as.

2 The *SWAY* circle represents the words *as we* in such phrases as:

as we have, as we think, as we shall, as we wish, as we may,

as we know, as we can, as we are. Note: *as well as*.

3 The large circle represents the two *s*'s in such phrases as:

this is, this is the, this city, as soon as, as soon as possible,

on this subject.

Intersections

Th represents *month*: .... *for the month*

    or *authority*: .... *my authority*

M represents *morning*: .... *Monday morning*

    or *manager*: .... *sales manager*

    or *market*: .... *market research*

Short form and phrasing practice

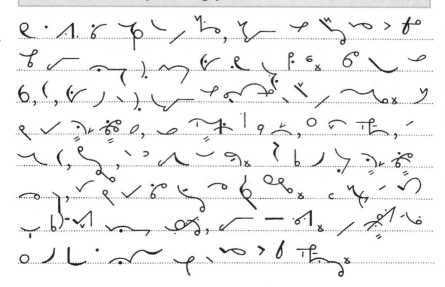

Practical dictation

1 **Memo to: All Staff**   **From: WP Supervisor**
   Subject: File codifying   **Date: Today's**

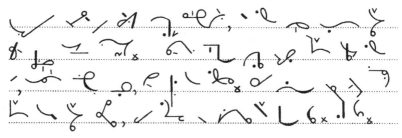

2 **Extract from an article on the value of exercise**

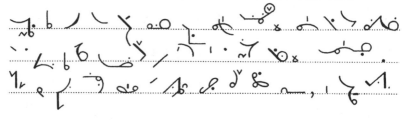

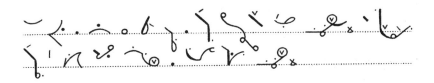

3 Letter regarding appointment of Research Manager

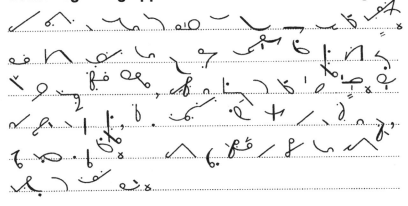

Theory check

Write the following in shorthand:

1 stereo
2 elastic
3 offices
4 statistics
5 refused

6 Swiss
7 necessary
8 barrister
9 cassette
10 pasta

Summary of the circles and loops

Loop/Circle	Beginning	Medial	End
S circle	such	basic	pass
STEE loop	state	justify	test
STER loop		masterpiece	register
SES circle		necessary	causes
SWAY circle	swing		

The circles and loops are written:

1 Inside curves
2 Anti-clockwise to straight strokes
3 Outside the angle created by two straight strokes

Unit 11
Halving

Strokes are halved to indicate a following *T* or *D*.

1 In words of *one* syllable a *light* stroke may be halved to indicate a
   following *T* only

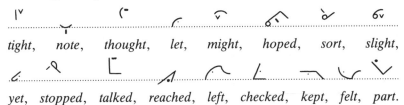

tight,   note,   thought,   let,   might,   hoped,   sort,   slight,

yet,   stopped,   talked,   reached,   left,   checked,   kept,   felt,   part.

Note: Half-length *H*, when not joined to another stroke, is always written
upward:

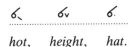

hot,   height,   hat.

2 In words of *one* syllable a *darker* stroke may be halved to indicate a
   following *D* only

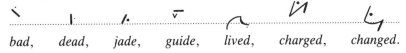

bad,   dead,   jade,   guide,   lived,   charged,   changed.

Note: The *S* circle is always read last:

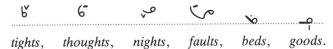

tights,   thoughts,   nights,   faults,   beds,   goods.

Reading and writing practice — 1

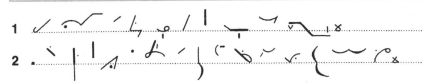

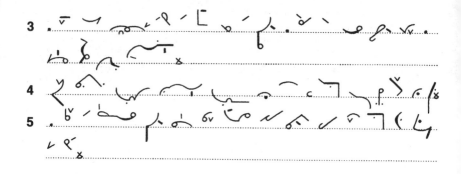

3 A stroke may be halved to indicate *either* a following *T* or *D*:

a in words of *more than* one syllable

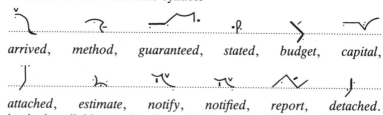

arrived,   method,   guaranteed,   stated,   budget,   capital,

attached,   estimate,   notify,   notified,   report,   detached.

b in single syllable words which have a final *joined* diphthong

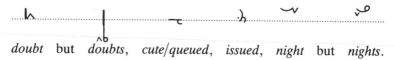

doubt but *doubts,   cute/queued,   issued,   night* but *nights.*

Notes:

a Half-length strokes are written on the line, not through the line, to indicate a third position:

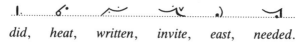

did,   heat,   written,   invite,   east,   needed.

b When *S-vowel-S* is followed by *T*, *S* circle is written initially so that the stroke *S* may be halved, eg ⟨⟩ *system.*

Reading and writing practice — 2

1

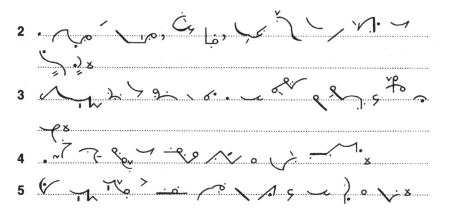

Halving and thickening

1 Strokes *M* and *N* are halved and thickened to indicate a following *D*

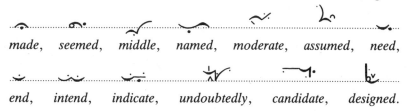

made,   seemed,   middle,   named,   moderate,   assumed,   need,

end,   intend,   indicate,   undoubtedly,   candidate,   designed.

2 Downward *L* and downward *R* are halved and thickened to indicate a following *D*

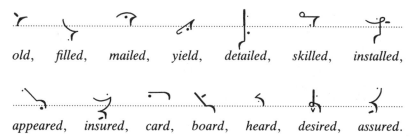

old,   filled,   mailed,   yield,   detailed,   skilled,   installed,

appeared,   insured,   card,   board,   heard,   desired,   assured.

3 If a sounded vowel comes between *L-D* or *R-D*, the full strokes must be written

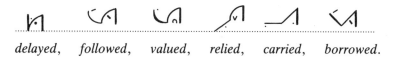

delayed,   followed,   valued,   relied,   carried,   borrowed.

Note: The halving system may be used in ordinal numbers:

21st, 22nd, 23rd.

Reading and writing practice — 3

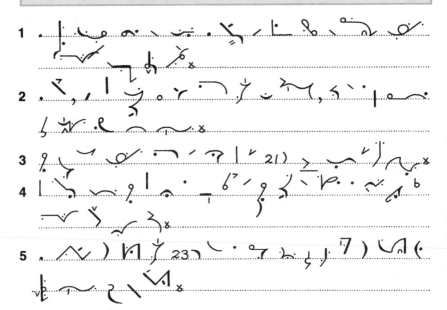

Non-use of halving

1 To avoid confusion with ⟋ *should* and ⟍ *and*, upward *R* is not halved when standing alone

rate, rights, writ, wrote, route/root, write.

2 In words where the length of a halved stroke would not clearly show, the halving principle is not used

fact, effect, locate, liked, select, minute, factory.

---

3 To be clearly shown, a half-length *T* or *D* must be disjoined following another *T* or *D*

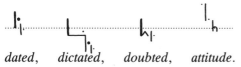

dated, dictated, doubted, attitude.

4 When a final vowel follows *T* or *D*, it is necessary to write the stroke in order to be able to place the vowel sign

pity, body, agenda, window, into.

Reading and writing practice — 4

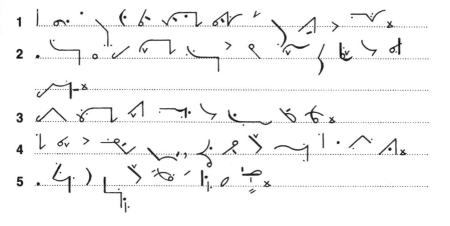

Short forms

quite, could, that, without, sent,

wished, hand, under, immediate, word,

certificate.

Phrases

The halving principle is used to indicate the words:

1 *it:*

if it,   if it is possible,   in which it is,   I think it is.

2 *word:*

few words,   in his own words.

3 *would:*

we would,   I would,   they would,   this would,   I would like.

4 *time:*

at the same time,   at some time,   for some time.

5 *out:*

carried out,   set out,   paid out.

Special phrases:

let us know,   let us have.

Intersections

N represents *national:*

national affairs,   National Bank

or *enquire/enquiry*
(inquire/inquiry):

we shall enquire,   your enquiry

Short form and phrasing practice

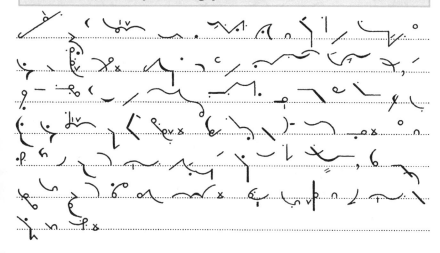

Practical dictation

1 The Works Manager leaves a message for his secretary

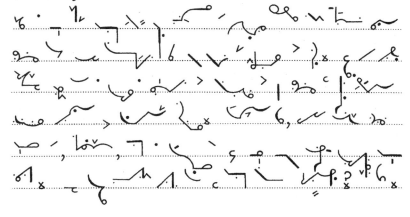

2 Factory Manager's report

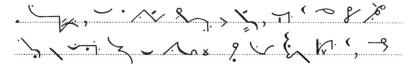

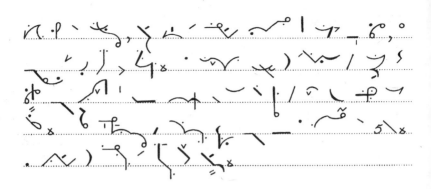

3 **Memo to: All Staff** **From: Managing Director**
Subject: New Packaging **Date: Today's**

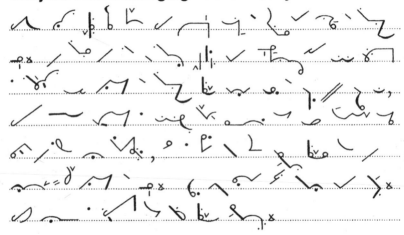

Write the following in shorthand:

1	thought	**6**	writing
2	report	**7**	dynamite
3	moved	**8**	married
4	assumed	**9**	solid
5	thousand	**10**	if it is

Unit 12
R Hook

Straight strokes

A small initial hook, written on the non-circle side of straight downstrokes and *K* and *G*, adds *R*. The small hook is written at the beginning of the stroke to the right (with a clockwise motion):

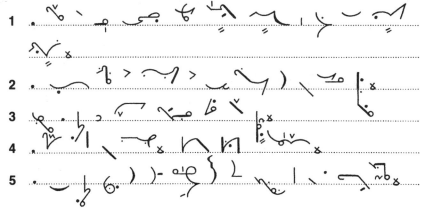

pr,   br,   tr,   dr,   chr,   jr,   kr,   gr.

(These are called *per*, *ber*, etc, though they do not always represent these syllables.)

April, October, trial, address, teacher, manager, increased, progress.

Reading and writing practice — 1

1

2

3

4

5

The sound of *R* is included:

1   When *S* circle is written in the *R* hook place

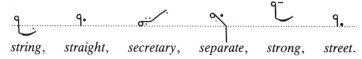

string,   straight,   secretary,   separate,   strong,   street.

2 When *ST* loop and *SWAY* circle are written in the *R* hook place

sticker,   stopper,   stagger   and   sweeper,   sweeter,   swagger.

3 However, *both* the *hook* and *circle* are shown when written in the middle of a word — write a small circle inside the hook

extra,   extremely,   industry,   district,   express.

4 When *SKR* or *SGR* follows *T* or *D* (the circle is written to the left — anti-clockwise)

describe,   discredit,   disagree.

Distinctive outlines: ___ *propriety*, ___ *property*;
___ *propose*, ___ *purpose*.

Reading and writing practice — 2

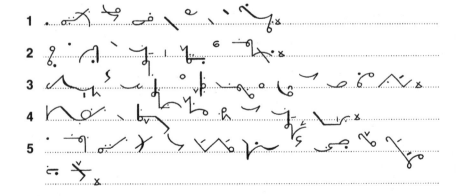

1

2

3

4

5

Special use of R hook with vowels

To promote writing speed, in some words the *R* hook is used even though there is a distinct vowel sound between the consonant and *R*.

1 Dot vowels may be replaced by a small circle as shown

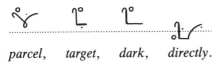

parcel,   target,   dark,   directly.

2 However, it is not necessary to indicate the short *e* vowel in words like

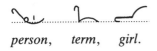

person,   term,   girl.

3 A *dash* vowel, or a *diphthong*, is shown by writing the vowel or diphthong sign at the beginning or end of the stroke, or through it

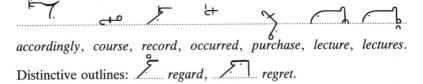

accordingly,   course,   record,   occurred,   purchase,   lecture,   lectures.

Distinctive outlines: ⟋ *regard,* ⟋⎺⎸ *regret.*

Reading and writing practice — 3

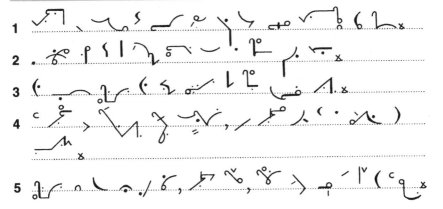

Short forms

⌐ doctor/Dr, ⌐ dear, ⌐ during, ⌐ truth, ⌐ larger, ⌐ principal/principally/principle, ⌐ care, ⌐ cared, ⌐ chair, ⌐ chaired, ⌐ liberty, ⌐ member/remember/remembered, ⌐ number/numbered, ⌐ description, ⌐ surprise, ⌐ surprised, ⌐ project/projected.

Phrases

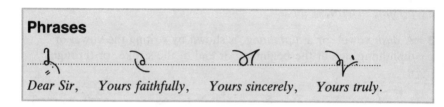

Dear Sir,   Yours faithfully,   Yours sincerely,   Yours truly.

Short form and phrase drill — 1

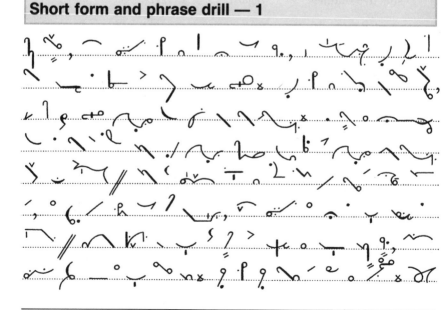

Curves

1 A small initial hook written on the inside of curves adds *R*

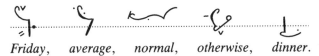

Friday,   average,   normal,   otherwise,   dinner.

2 *S* may be added at the beginning of a curved stroke by writing a small *S* circle inside the *R* hook

sooner,   summer,   safer.

Note: The intervening diphone is written through the hooked stroke in a few words:

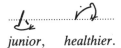

junior,   healthier.

3 As well as the forms ⌒ FR, ⌒ VR, (Thr, (THR,

reverse forms ⌐ FR, ⌐ VR,) Thr,) THR,

are written when:

a the word does not begin with a vowel, and
b this is the only stroke in the word.

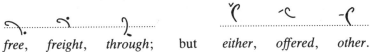

free,   freight,   through;   but   *either,   offered,   other.*

Reading and writing practice — 4

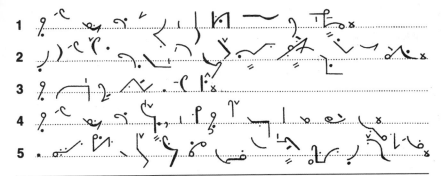

4 However, when joined to another stroke, the most convenient writing form is used to give the clearest outline — for example reverse forms are usually joined to strokes written towards the right

before, discover, cover, forgot, gather, Thursday, fresh.

5 The stroke *SHR* is always written downwards as in ⟶ *pressure.*

6 *R* hook is added to *NG* ⟶ to represent *NG-KR* or *NG-GR*

banker, stronger.

Reading and writing practice — 5

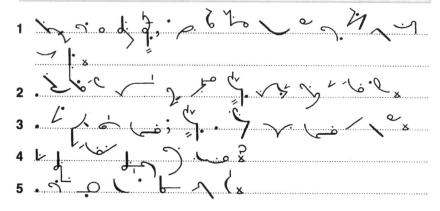

Short forms

⟶ *nor,* ⟶ *near,* ⟶ *more/remark/remarked,* ⟶ *accord/according,* ⟶ *Mr/mere,* ⟶ *sure,* ⟶ *pleasure,* ⟶ *short,* ⟶ *over,* ⟶ *however,* ⟶ *from,* ⟶ *very,* ⟶ *their/there.*

Phrases

1 *according:*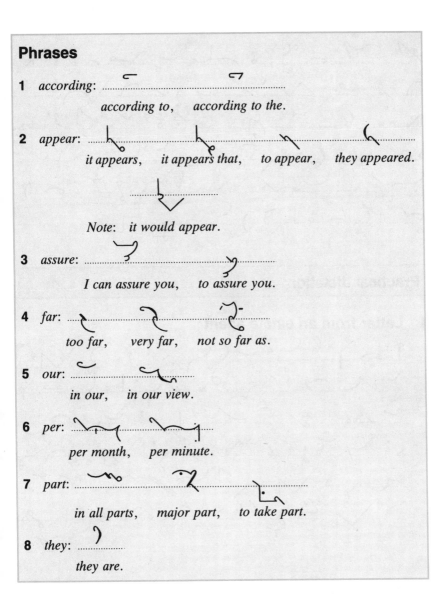

        according to,   according to the.

2 *appear:*

        it appears,   it appears that,   to appear,   they appeared.

        Note: it would appear.

3 *assure:*

        I can assure you,   to assure you.

4 *far:*

        too far,   very far,   not so far as.

5 *our:*

        in our,   in our view.

6 *per:*

        per month,   per minute.

7 *part:*

        in all parts,   major part,   to take part.

8 *they:*

        they are.

Short form and phrasing practice — 2

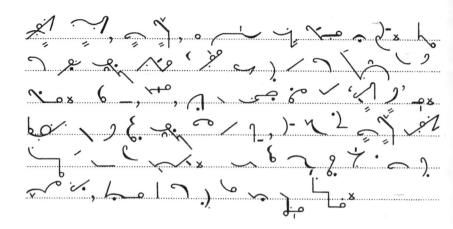

Practical dictation

1 Letter from an estate agent

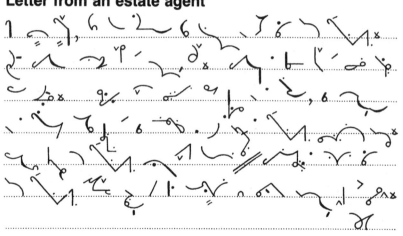

2 Letter about a new range of goods for sale

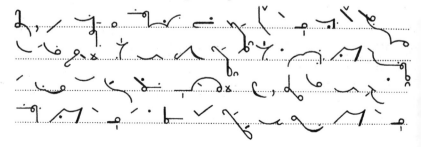

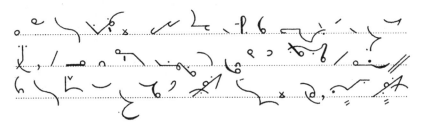

3 Letter from a freight transport company

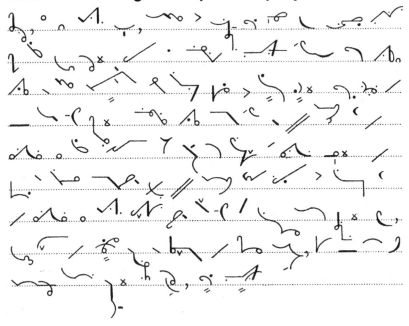

Write the following in shorthand:

1 programme
2 strength
3 disgrace
4 literature
5 everybody

6 forgot
7 conquer
8 street
9 direct
10 attorney

Unit 13
N Hook

1 A small final hook, written on the inside of curves, adds *N*

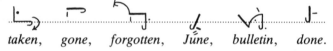

often, 'phone, then, machine, salesman, loan.

2 At the end of all straight strokes the *N* hook is written to the right (in a clockwise direction)

taken, gone, forgotten, June, bulletin, done.

3 When *N* hook follows *R* at the end of a word, the *R* is usually written upwards

turn, return, learn, western, corn, pattern.

Reading and writing practice — 1

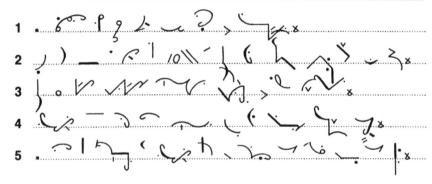

4 A finally hooked stroke is halved to indicate a following *T* or *D*

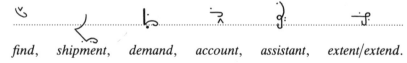

find, shipment, demand, account, assistant, extent/extend.

5 *N* hook is used in the middle of an outline when it joins easily to the following stroke

training,   attended,   arrangement,   merchandise,   correspondence,

standing;

but not in cases where the *N* hook does not join easily to a following stroke

wanted,   printed,   meantime,   seconded,   accounted.

Reading and writing practice — 2

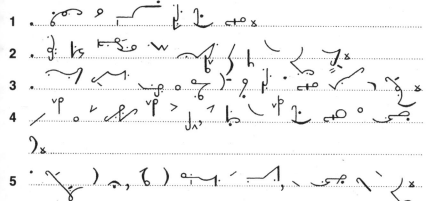

1

2

3

4

5

6 On all straight strokes a final circle or loop written on the *N* hook side, includes the *N*

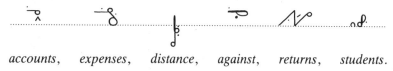

accounts,   expenses,   distance,   against,   returns,   students.

7 After a curved stroke:

   a The light sound *-NCE* is written using stroke *N* and the appropriate circle or loop

announce,   announces,   announced,   announcing.

   b In full length curves a circle written inside the hook adds the final sound of *NZ* only

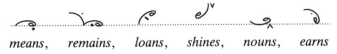

means,   remains,   loans,   shines,   nouns,   earns

   c In *half-length* curves a circle written inside the hook adds the final sound of *S* or *Z*

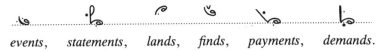

events,   statements,   lands,   finds,   payments,   demands.

8 *N* hook is not used when a vowel ends a word. In these cases it is necessary to write the stroke to indicate the vowel

county but *count*;   *many* but *men*;   *funny* but *fun*;   *penny* but *pen*.

Reading and writing practice — 3

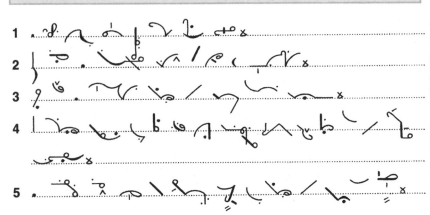

Short forms

.... been, ... general/generally, ... within, ... southern, ... northern, ... opinion, ... own, ... owner, ... expenditure, ... expensive, ... organise/organised.

Phrases

1 *N*-hook may be used to represent the following words in phrasing

been:
> had been,   have been.

than:
> more than,   better than,   larger than,   smaller than.

next:
> Wednesday next.

on:
> going on,   carried on.

once:
> at once.

own:
> our own,   their own.

2 *not* may be represented by halving a stroke for *T* and adding *N* hook:

> I am not,   you are not,   you will not,   did not,

> had not/do not,   cannot,   they are not.

Short form and phrasing practice

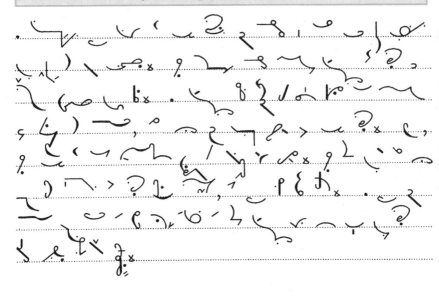

Practical dictation

1 Letter to Personnel Manager regarding work experience placements

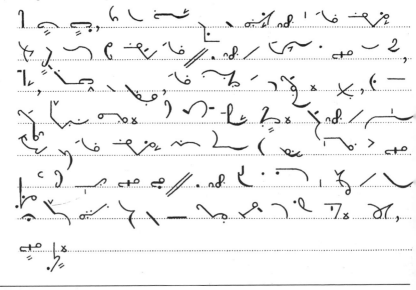

2 Memorandum to Reprographics Manager

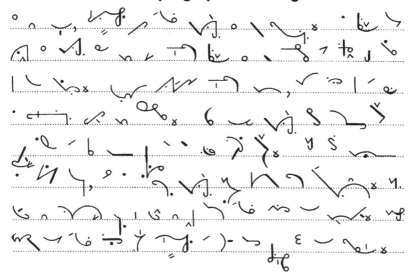

3 Letter about the opening of a new factory

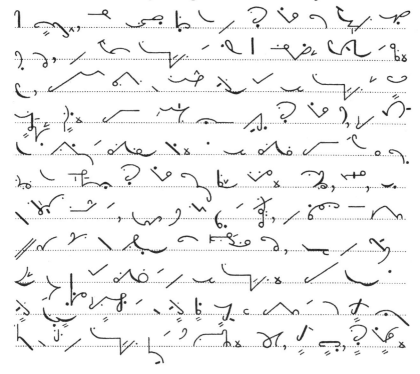

Write the following in shorthand:

1 known
2 drawn
3 movement
4 current
5 extended

6 spending
7 country
8 stands
9 fenced
10 lines

Unit 14

WH, Abbreviated W, WL, WHL, and Medial W

WH

The upstroke ⟨image⟩ is the most common method of representing the consonant *WAY*, as already seen

west,   went,   once,   weather,   awake,   Wednesday,   wood.

H is added to ⟨image⟩ by enlarging the hook ⟨image⟩ *WH*

where,   everywhere,   somewhere,   elsewhere,   white,

whistle,   wherever,   whereabouts,   whisper.

Reading and writing practice — 1

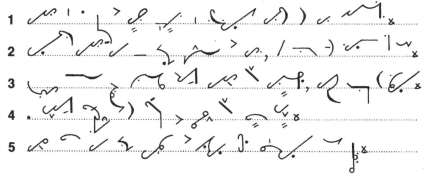

1

2

3

4

5

Abbreviated W

A small semicircle, written as shown, is used as an abbreviation for *W* before *K, G, M,* and upward and downward *R*

week,   wagon,   woman,   women,   warden,   warehouse,   warrant,   worth, *warranty, world, worried, work, were, warm, warn, wire, worst.*

Note: When a word begins vowel-*W*, the stroke *W* must be written:

wake but *awake*;   *ware* but *aware*;   *ward* but *award*.

Reading and writing practice — 2

1

2

3

4

5

WL, WHL

1 *WL* is represented by writing a small hook inside upward *L*

will,   well,   wealthy,   unwilling,   welfare,   well-being.

2 *WHL* is represented by writing a large hook inside upward *L*

while,   whilst,   wheel,   meanwhile.

Medial W

In the middle of a word, where stroke *WAY* would be difficult to write, *W* can be represented by the abbreviated *W*, which is written in the position of the following vowel.

1 A left semicircle represents *W* followed by a *dot* vowel

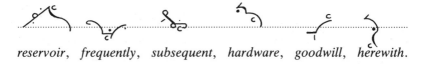

reservoir, frequently, subsequent, hardware, goodwill, herewith.

2 A right semicircle represents *W* followed by a *dash* vowel

woodwork, waterworks, someone.

Special outline:  *somewhat.*

Reading and writing practice — 3

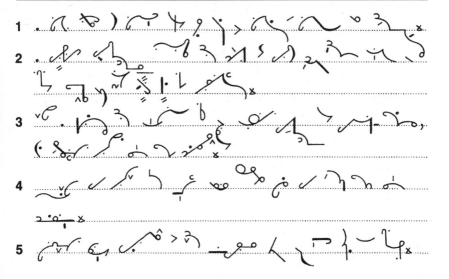

Vowel indication

Vowel omission was introduced in Unit 6 for outlines where stroke *S* is written. You will now find that the various rules you are learning will make it possible for you to write outlines which are so clearly distinctive that it is unnecessary to insert the vowel signs. The omission of vowels emphasises the importance of accurate position writing. Correct position writing enables most vowels to be omitted, and this is a great speed builder.

From now on we shall insert only the essential vowels needed to ensure quick and accurate reading back of shorthand notes.

Short forms

✗ *respect/respected,* ✗ *expect/expected,* ✗ *inspect/inspected/ inspection,* ⟶ *together,* ⟶ *altogether,* ⟶ *insurance,* ⟶ *practice/practise/practised,* ⟶ *university,* ⟶ *exchange/ exchanged,* ⟶ *familiar/familiarity,* ⟶ *whether.*

Phrases

1 *were*:

you were, you were not, who were, which were, they were, we were.

2 *week*:

this week,   next week,   last week,   3 weeks,   6 weeks.

3 *will*:

will not,   and will,   we will.

Other phrases:

very well,   worth while,   stock exchange,   throughout the world.

Intersection

Intersected *G* hooked for *N* represents *beginning*:

at the beginning,   by the beginning,   from the beginning.

Short form and phrasing practice

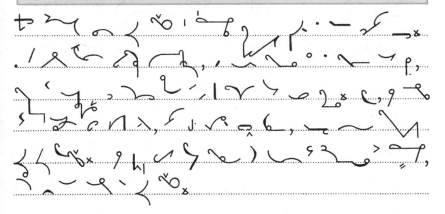

Practical dictation

1 Letter of enquiry

2 Reply to letter of enquiry

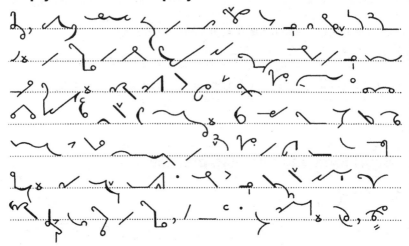

3 Extract from newspaper article

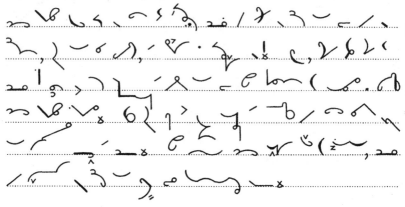

Theory check

Write the following in shorthand:

1	where	6	meanwhile
2	warehouse	7	framework
3	weaken	8	who were not
4	warm	9	6 weeks
5	unwell	10	aware

Unit 15
L Hook

A small initial hook written on the *S* circle side of straight downstrokes and *K* and *G* adds the sound of *L*. The small hook is written at the beginning of the stroke to the left (in an anti-clockwise direction):

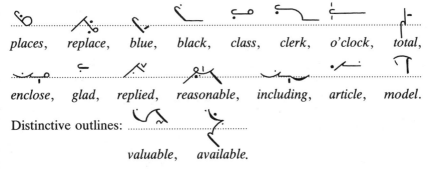

pl,   bl,   tl,   dl,   chl,   jl,   kl,   gl.

(These are called *pel*, *bel*, etc, though they do not always represent these syllables.)

places,   replace,   blue,   black,   class,   clerk,   o'clock,   total,

enclose,   glad,   replied,   reasonable,   including,   article,   model.

Distinctive outlines: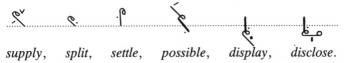

valuable,   available.

1   The *S* circle is written inside the hook, whether used at the beginning or in the middle of an outline

supply,   split,   settle,   possible,   display,   disclose.

Note: If the *S* circle is written at the beginning of an outline, it is always read first.

Reading and writing practice — 1

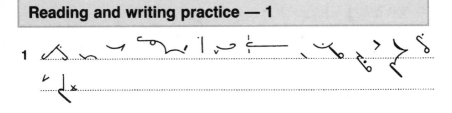

1

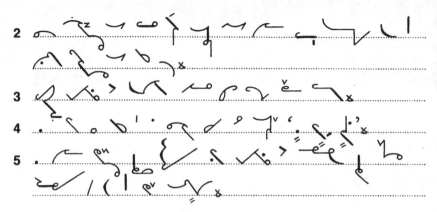

2 A large initial hook, written on the inside of certain curves, adds the sound of *L*

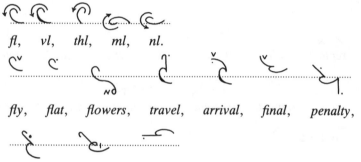

fl, *vl,* *thl,* *ml,* *nl.*

fly, *flat,* *flowers,* *travel,* *arrival,* *final,* *penalty,*

playful, *personal,* *camel.*

3 The circle S at the beginning of the outline is written inside the hook and is always read first, eg ...ℰ... *civil.*

Reading and writing practice — 2

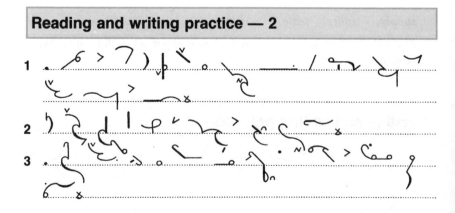

4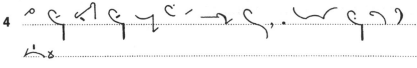

5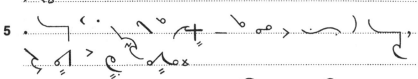

4 After *K*, *G*, *N* or a straight upstroke, 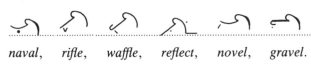 *FL* and *VL* are reversed: and .

naval, rifle, waffle, reflect, novel, gravel.

1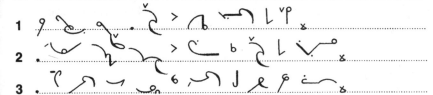

2

3

4

5

5 The double consonant stroke *SHL* is always written upwards:

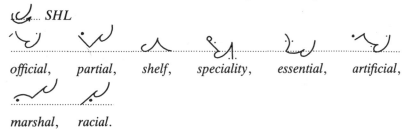 *SHL*

official, partial, shelf, speciality, essential, artificial,

marshal, racial.

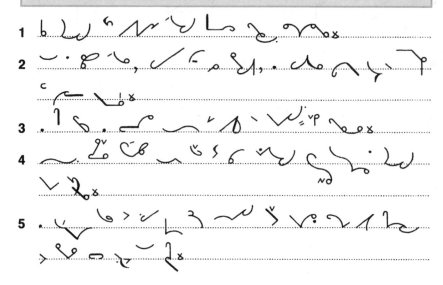

Special use of L hook with vowels

To promote writing speed, in some words the *L* hook is used even though a distinct vowel comes between the consonant and *L*.

1 Dot vowels may be replaced by writing a small circle before or after the stroke hooked for *L*

challenge,   children.

2 Where the intervening vowel is the short *e*, no vowel sign is written

delightful,   delicate,   telegraphy,   delegate,   telex.

3 A dash vowel or a diphthong is shown by writing the vowel or diphthong sign at the beginning or the end of the stroke, or through it.

political,   nullify,   tolerate,   fulfil,   collect,   college.

4 In words of *one* syllable, where a vowel occurs between the consonant and the *L*, the hooked stroke generally is not used

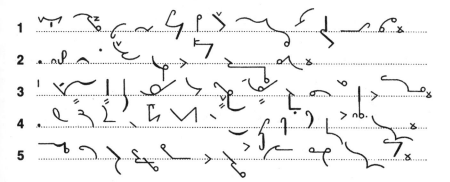

fly but *fall*;   *blow* but *ball*;   *play* but *pill*.

Reading and writing practice — 5

1
2
3
4
5

Short forms

⟍ *equal/equally,* ⟍ *equalled/cold,* ⟍ *people,* ⟍ *belief/ believe/believed,* ⎰ *tell,* ⎰ *deliver/delivery/delivered,* ⎰ *telegram,* ⎰ *largely,* ⌒ *call,* ⌒ *called,* ⟍ *build/ building,* ⟍ *balance,* ⟍ *balanced,* ⟍ *distinguish/distinguished,* ⟍ *nevertheless,* ⟍ *remarkable.*

Phrases

1 *all*:

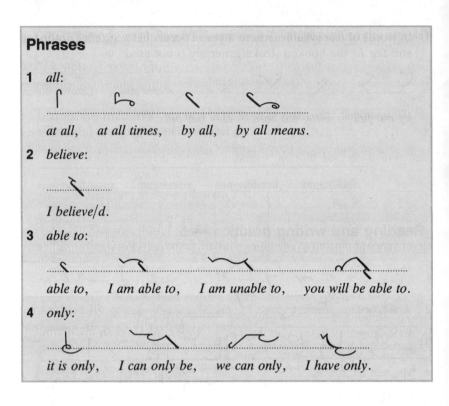

at all,   at all times,   by all,   by all means.

2 *believe*:

I believe/d.

3 *able to*:

able to,   I am able to,   I am unable to,   you will be able to.

4 *only*:

it is only,   I can only be,   we can only,   I have only.

Short form and phrasing practice

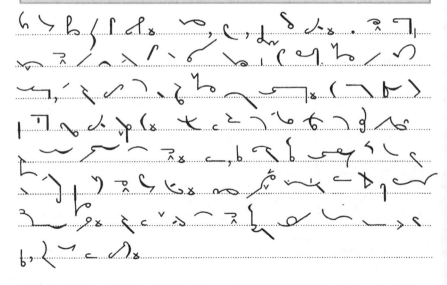

1 Letter regarding a home for the disabled

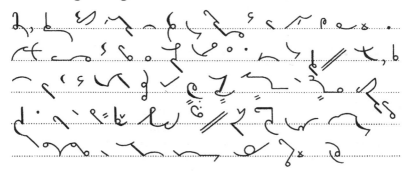

2 Letter from an insurance company following a burglary

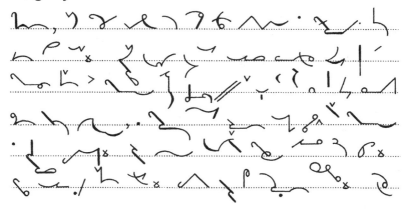

3 A reply to an enquiry regarding floor tiles

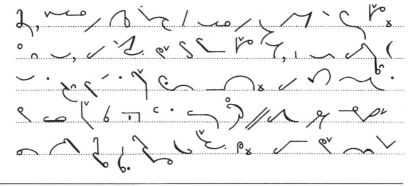

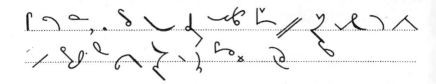

Write the following in shorthand:

1	reasonable	6	roughly
2	article	7	athletics
3	hopefully	8	inflict
4	cyclist	9	gravely
5	developed	10	bicycle

A small final hook, written with a left (anti-clockwise) motion at the end of all straight strokes adds *F* or *V*

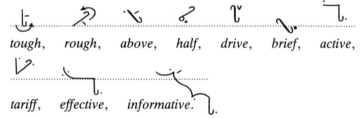

tough,   rough,   above,   half,   drive,   brief,   active,

tariff,   effective,   informative.

Note: When a vowel follows *F* or *V* at the end of a word, it is necessary to write the stroke to indicate the following vowel:

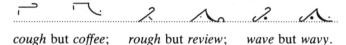

cough but *coffee*;   rough but *review*;   wave but *wavy*.

There is no F/V hook to curves.

Reading and writing practice — 1

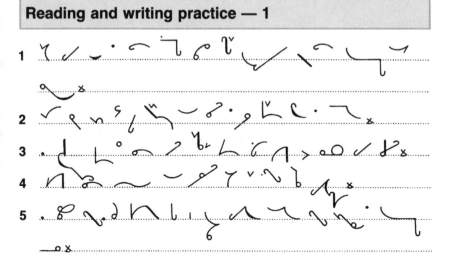

A finally hooked stroke is halved to indicate a following *T* or *D*

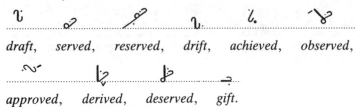

draft,   served,   reserved,   drift,   achieved,   observed,

approved,   derived,   deserved,   gift.

Reading and writing practice — 2

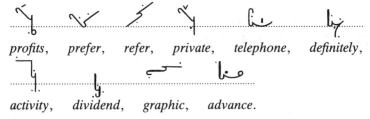

1
2
3
4
5

The *F/V* hook is used in the middle of an outline when it joins easily to the following stroke

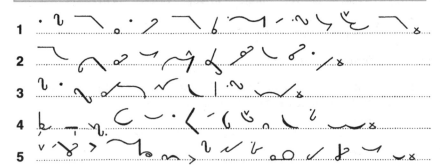

profits,   prefer,   refer,   private,   telephone,   definitely,

activity,   dividend,   graphic,   advance.

Reading and writing practice — 3

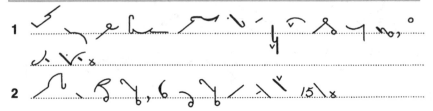

1

2

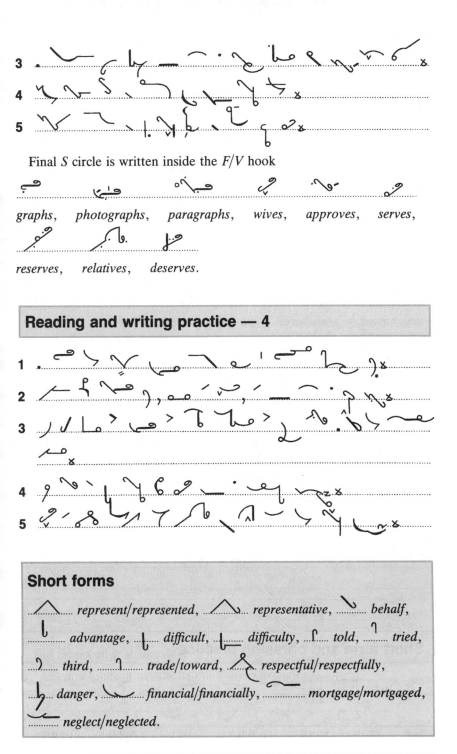

3 ....

4 ....

5 ....

Final *S* circle is written inside the *F/V* hook

graphs,   photographs,   paragraphs,   wives,   approves,   serves,

reserves,   relatives,   deserves.

Reading and writing practice — 4

1 ....

2 ....

3 ....

....

4 ....

5 ....

Short forms

represent/represented,   representative,   behalf,

advantage,   difficult,   difficulty,   told,   tried,

third,   trade/toward,   respectful/respectfully,

danger,   financial/financially,   mortgage/mortgaged,

neglect/neglected.

Phrases

F/V hook can be used for the addition of the following words:

1 *of*:

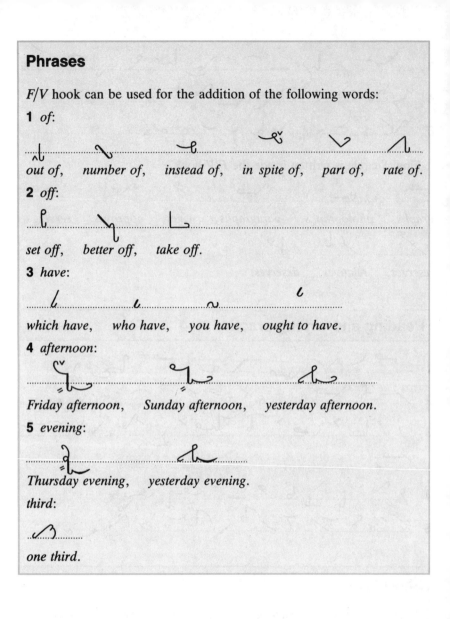

out of,　number of,　instead of,　in spite of,　part of,　rate of.

2 *off*:

set off,　better off,　take off.

3 *have*:

which have,　who have,　you have,　ought to have.

4 *afternoon*:

Friday afternoon,　Sunday afternoon,　yesterday afternoon.

5 *evening*:

Thursday evening,　yesterday evening.

third:

one third.

Short form and phrasing practice

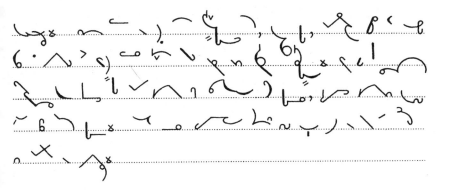

1 Extract from an annual report to shareholders

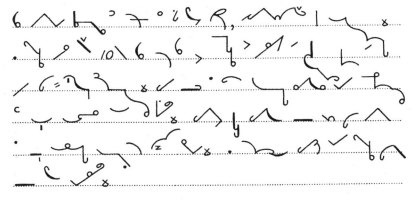

2 Building society letter regarding a mortgage advance

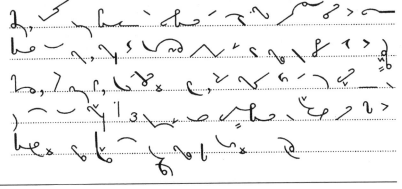

3 Extract from an article on the 'Black Economy'

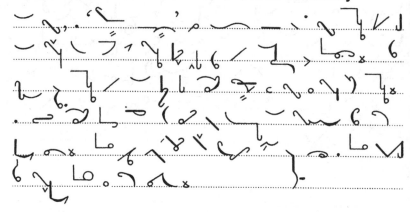

Write the following in shorthand:

1	above	6	divide
2	overdraft	7	photographic
3	perfect	8	Thursday afternoon
4	province	9	alternative
5	drives	10	photography

Unit 17
SHUN Hook; upward SH

A large final hook to a stroke adds the sound of *SHUN*.

Curved strokes:

1 The *SHUN* hook is written inside a curve

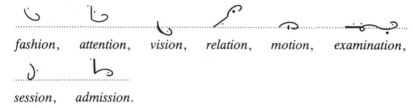

fashion,   attention,   vision,   relation,   motion,   examination,

session,   admission.

2 The *S* circle may be added to the *SHUN* hook, and is read last

observations,   missions,   nations.

3 The *SHUN* hook can also be used in the middle of an outline if it gives an easy joining

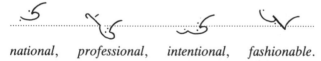

national,   professional,   intentional,   fashionable.

Reading and writing practice — 1

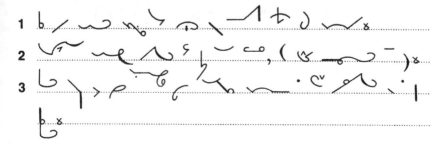

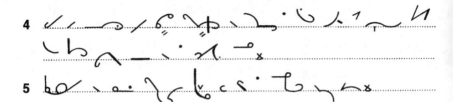

4 ....

....

5 ....

Straight strokes:

1 When attached to a straight stroke the *SHUN* hook is written on the side opposite to an initial hook or circle to balance the outline

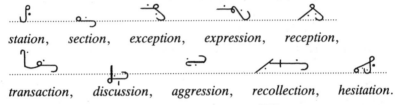

station,   section,   exception,   expression,   reception,

transaction,   discussion,   aggression,   recollection,   hesitation.

2 After ⌐⌐⌐ *F-K*, ⌐⌐⌐ *V-K/G* and ⌐⌐⌐ *L-K/G*, the *SHUN* hook is written away from the curve to balance the outline

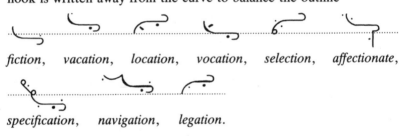

fiction,   vacation,   location,   vocation,   selection,   affectionate,

specification,   navigation,   legation.

Reading and writing practice — 2

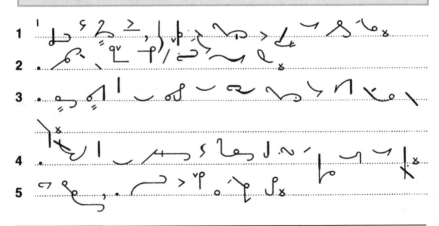

1 ....

2 ....

3 ....

....

4 ....

5 ....

3 The SHUN hook is written on the right side of *T*, *D*, or *J* when these strokes have no initial circle or hook

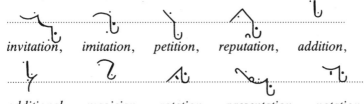

invitation,   *imitation,*   *petition,*   *reputation,*   *addition,*

additional,   *magician,*   *rotation,*   *presentation,*   *notation.*

4 When added to other simple straight strokes, *SHUN* is written on the side opposite the last vowel

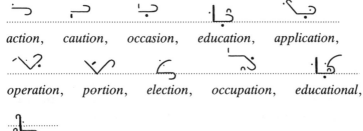

action,   *caution,*   *occasion,*   *education,*   *application,*

operation,   *portion,*   *election,*   *occupation,*   *educational,*

direction.

5 A stroke hooked for *SHUN* may be halved to indicate a final *T* or *D*

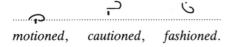

motioned,   *cautioned,*   *fashioned.*

Note: As can be seen from the examples given in this unit:

a A third-place dot vowel is written inside the *SHUN* hook.

b A third-place dash vowel or diphthong *U* is written inside *SHUN* hook if this comes in the middle of a word, but otherwise it is written outside *SHUN* in the usual way.

vision,   *addition,*   *application,*   *educational* but *education.*

Reading and writing practice — 3

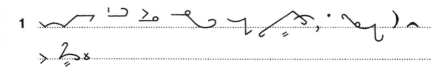

1

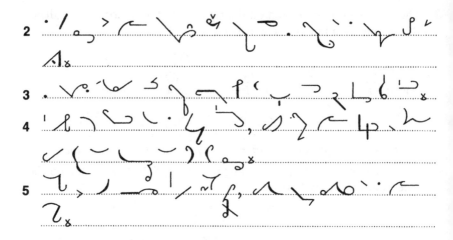

2 ....

3 ....

4 ....

5 ....

S-SHUN

1 When *SHUN* follows the *S* circle or the *NS* circle, it is represented by a small curl written in the same direction (a continuation of the circle).

2 A third-place vowel between the *S* and the *SHUN* is placed outside the curl. Any other vowel is not indicated.

3 A final *S* circle can be written inside the curl.

Note: *L* may be added for derivatives eg *sensational*.

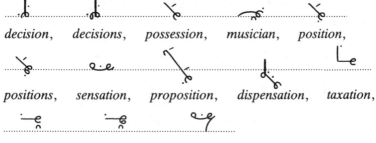

decision,   decisions,   possession,   musician,   position,

positions,   sensation,   proposition,   dispensation,   taxation,

accusation,   accusations,   sensational.

4 In words ending in *-UATION* or *-UITION* the stroke *SH* and *N* hook are generally written

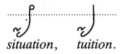

situation,   tuition.

Reading and writing practice — 4

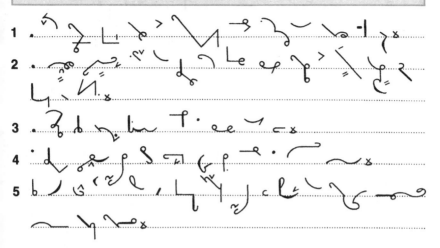

Upward SH

Though *SH* is generally written downwards ...𝐽𝐽.., in certain cases it is written upwards ...𝐽𝑇.. to obtain an outline that is easier to write and to read

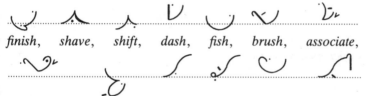

finish,   shave,   shift,   dash,   fish,   brush,   associate,

appreciation,   foolish,   shell,   social,   flash,   shoulder.

Note: Where it would be unclear if the stroke were halved for *T* or *D*, *SHUN* hook is replaced by *SH* and *N* hook:

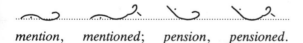

mention,   mentioned;   *pension,   pensioned.*

Reading and writing practice — 5

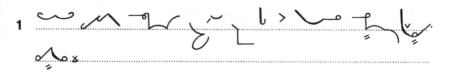

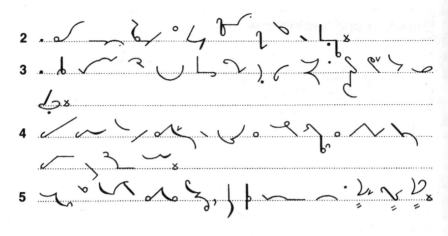

2 ...
3 ...
4 ...
5 ...

Short forms

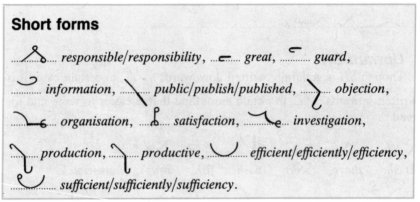

responsible/responsibility, great, guard, information, public/publish/published, objection, organisation, satisfaction, investigation, production, productive, efficient/efficiently/efficiency, sufficient/sufficiently/sufficiency.

Phrases

Association:

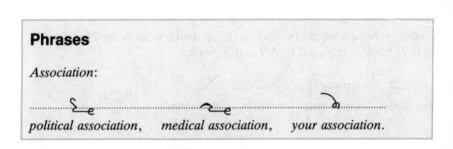

political association,   medical association,   your association.

Short form and phrasing practice

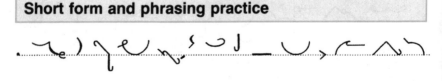

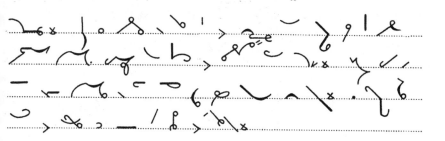

Practical dictation

1 Letter regarding a statement in the press

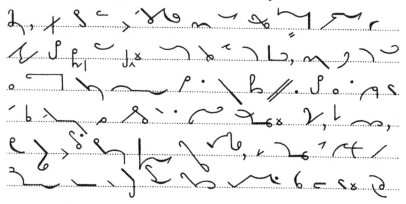

2 Letter to a removal firm

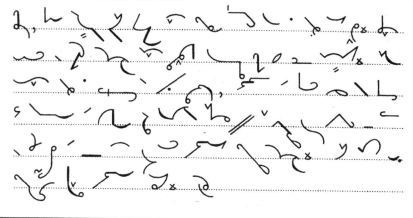

3 **Memo to: Managing Director**   **From: Personnel Manager**
Subject: John Taylor   **Date: Today's**

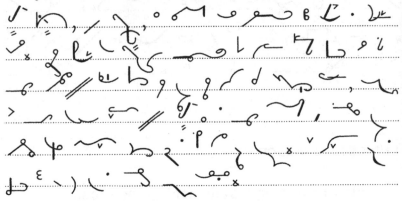

Write the following in shorthand:

1 additional	**6** auction
2 appreciated	**7** edition
3 notification	**8** musicians
4 educational	**9** sugar
5 resolutions	**10** dish

Unit 18
Compound consonants and the omission of consonants

Compound consonants

The compound consonants are as follows:

Letter	Sign	Name	As in		
KW	⟋	kwa	quick	request	question
GW	⟍	gwa	linguist	language	bilingual
MP, MB	⌒	emp} emb}	camp	impose	embassy
LR	⟨	ler	filler	ruler	chancellor
RR	⟍	rer	poorer	admirer	clearer

Note: Compound consonants WL, WH and WHL were introduced in Unit 14.

1 *KW* and *GW*

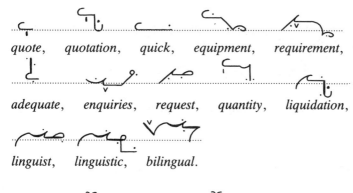

quote, quotation, quick, equipment, requirement,

adequate, enquiries, request, quantity, liquidation,

linguist, linguistic, bilingual.

Special outlines:

quality, qualified, qualification.

Reading and writing practice — 1

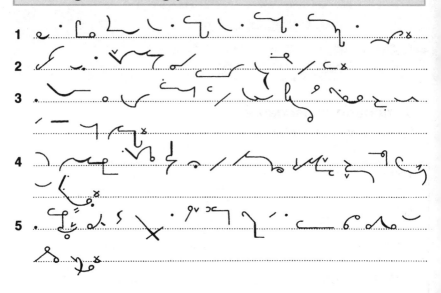

2 *MP, MB*

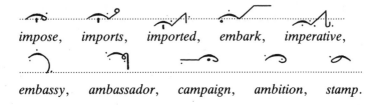

impose, imports, imported, embark, imperative,

embassy, ambassador, campaign, ambition, stamp.

Note: When *M* is immediately followed by *PR, BR, PL* or *BL*, the hooks  are used:

impress, umbrella, imply, emblem.

3 *LR*
Ler can only be used where downward *L* would be written

rule and *ruler;   full* and *fuller;   council* and *councillor;   scholar.*

4 RR

Rer can only be used where downward *R* would be written

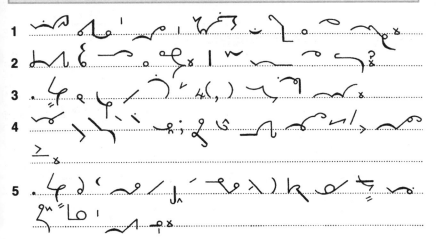

poor and *poorer*; *clear* and *clearer*; *admire* and *admirer*.

Reading and writing practice — 2

1
2
3
4
5

Consonant omission

1 A lightly sounded *T* in the middle of a word, if following *S* circle, may sometimes be omitted

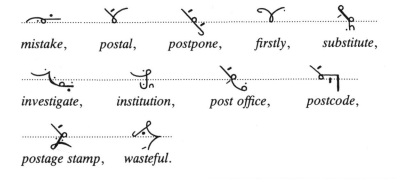

mistake,   postal,   postpone,   firstly,   substitute,

investigate,   institution,   post office,   postcode,

postage stamp,   wasteful.

2 Other lightly sounded consonants are omitted in some words

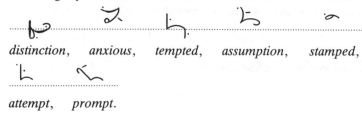

distinction,   anxious,   tempted,   assumption,   stamped,

attempt,   prompt.

Reading and writing practice — 3

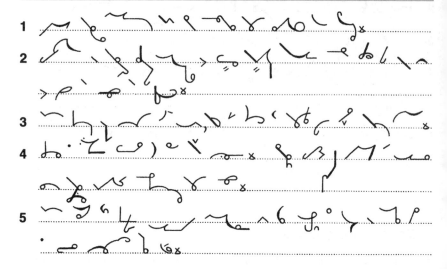

Phrases

In many common phrases, consonants, syllables or whole words may be omitted. These phrases should be quick to write and also easy to read back. You have already met some phrases with omissions.

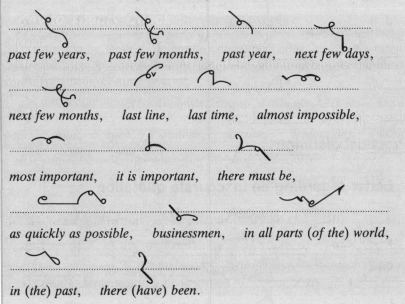

past few years,   *past few months,*   *past year,*   *next few days,*

next few months,   *last line,*   *last time,*   *almost impossible,*

most important,   *it is important,*   *there must be,*

as quickly as possible,   *businessmen,*   *in all parts (of the) world,*

in (the) past,   *there (have) been.*

Intersections

KR represents *corporation*:   .... *public corporation.*

P + L + S circle represents *plc*: .... *Hi-tech Business Systems plc.*

Short form and phrasing practice

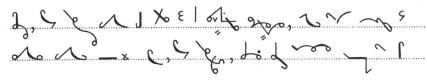

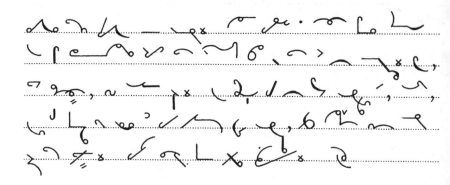

Practical dictation

1 Letter regarding an inaccurate quotation

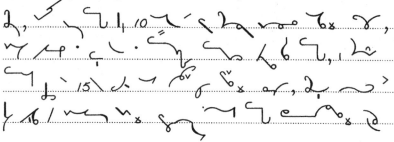

2 Memo to: Secretarial Staff From: Post room Supervisor
Subject: Addressing envelopes Date: Today's

3 Advertisement for a bilingual secretary

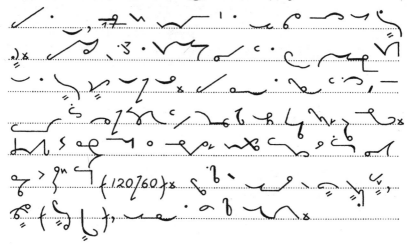

Write the following in shorthand:

1 question
2 multi-lingual
3 temporary
4 embezzler
5 language

6 imposition
7 investigate
8 distinct
9 fuller
10 implication

Unit 19
Doubling

1 Curved strokes are doubled in length to indicate a following syllable *TER*, *DER*, *THer* (heavy sound), and, in a few common words, *TURE*. All double length downstrokes are written through the line.

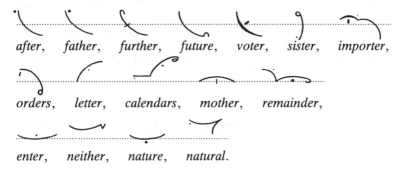

after,   father,   further,   future,   voter,   sister,   importer,

orders,   letter,   calendars,   mother,   remainder,

enter,   neither,   nature,   natural.

2 Stroke *L*, standing alone or with only a final *S* circle, is doubled for *TER* only

litter,   alters,   latter but *leader,   older,   leather.*

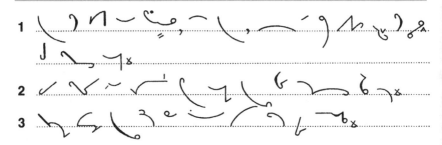

1

2

3

4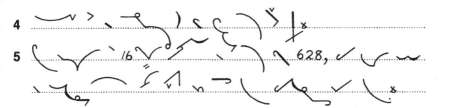

5

3 Straight strokes are doubled for the addition of *TER*, *DER*, *THer* and, in a few common words, *TURE*:

a When following another stroke

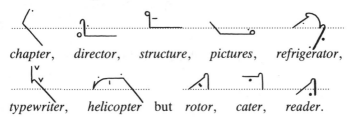

chapter, director, structure, pictures, refrigerator,

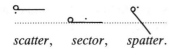

typewriter, helicopter but rotor, cater, reader.

b when following circle *S*

scatter, sector, spatter.

c when there is a finally joined diphthong

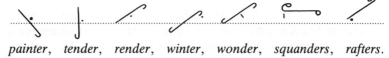

powder, pewter, tutor but powders, tutors.

d when there is a final hook or *NS* circle

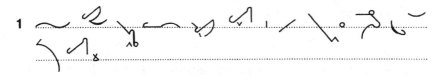

painter, tender, render, winter, wonder, squanders, rafters.

Reading and writing practice — 2

1

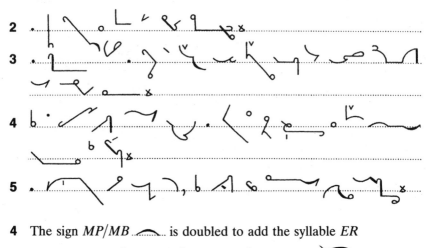

4 The sign *MP/MB*  is doubled to add the syllable *ER*

September,   December,   temper,   temperature,   sombre,   amber.

5 Another way to represent the sounds *MPER/MBER* is to use the hooked form ⌒ and this stroke is used following horizontals and upstrokes for a more easily written and legible outline

camper,   hamper,   lumber.

6 *NG* ⌣ is doubled to add the syllables *KER* or *GER*

anchor/anger,   longer,   linger,   hunger,   handkerchief.

As was seen in Unit 12, the hooked stroke ⌣ also represents the sounds *NG-KER/NG-GER* and this form is used following horizontals and downstrokes, for a more easily written and legible outline

conquer,   banker,   tanker,   finger,   stronger.

7 The doubling principle is not used:
a when there is a final vowel

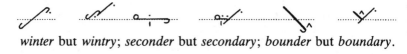

winter but *wintry*; *seconder* but *secondary*; *bounder* but *boundary*.

b in past tenses

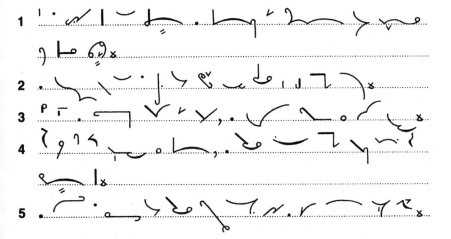

rendered, tendered, ordered, mattered, surrendered.

Reading and writing practice — 3

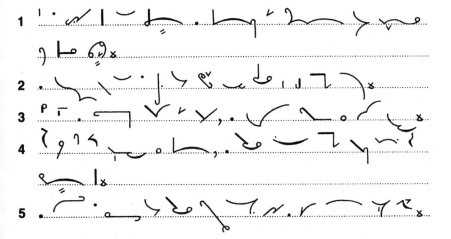

Short forms

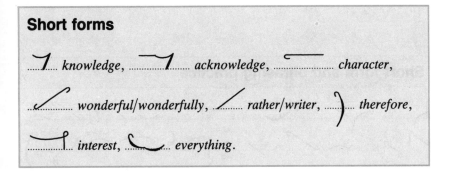

knowledge, acknowledge, character, wonderful/wonderfully, rather/writer, therefore, interest, everything.

Phrases

The doubling principle is used in phrases to add the words:

1 *there/their*:

in there/their,   from there/their,   if there is,   I think there is.

2 *other*:

some other,   in other words,   in other times.

but compare:

any/in other,   no other,   among other,   many other.

3 *order*:

in order,   in order that   Note: *in order to.*

Other phrases:

not later than,   no longer than,   any longer than,   rather than,

this letter,   as a matter of fact.

Short form and phrasing practice

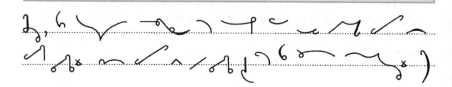

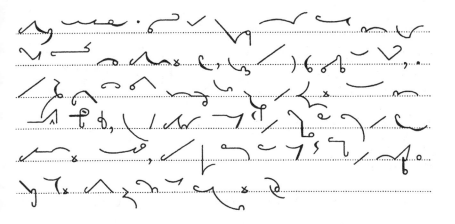

Practical dictation

1 Newspaper report of a road traffic accident

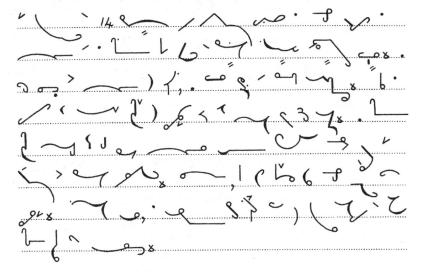

2 Business letter

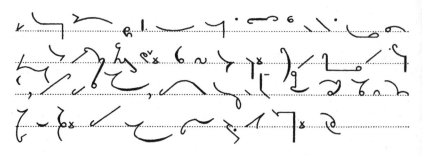

3 Circular

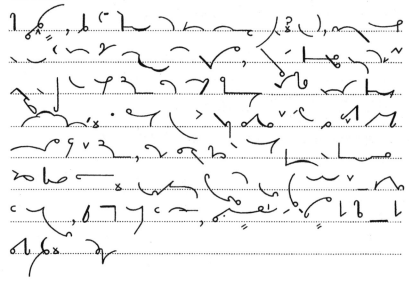

Theory check

Write the following in shorthand:

1	order	**6**	adventure
2	letter	**7**	holder
3	leather	**8**	dictator
4	ponder	**9**	hunger
5	sombre	**10**	going there

Unit 20
Prefixes, suffixes and word endings

Prefixes

1 A light dot written at the beginning of a stroke adds the sound of *CON/COM*. The first vowel after this prefix decides the outline's position.

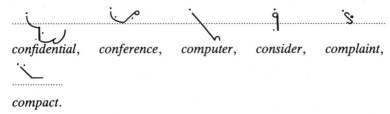

confidential,   conference,   computer,   consider,   complaint,

compact.

Two special outlines which you should memorise are

commerce,   commission.

CON-, *COM-*, *CUM-*, or *COG-* may be shown in the middle of a word by writing both parts of the word separately (disjoined) but close together

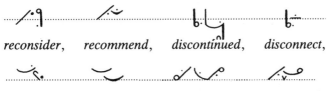

reconsider,   recommend,   discontinued,   disconnect,

incomplete,   incoming,   circumference,   recognise.

Note: After another word, the dot may be omitted if the two outlines can be written clearly close together. This cannot be done after *a*, *the*, or single downward dash short forms.

2 *ACCOM-* or *ACCOMMO-* is represented by the consonant *K*, either joined (*accomplish* and its derivatives, and *accommodation*) or disjoined, but written in first position (for vowel *a*)

accomplish,   accomplice,   accompanied,   accommodation.

3 *INTRO*- is represented by *NTR*, written in the third position (for vowel *i*)

introduce,   introvert.

4 *MAGNA-*, *MAGNE-*, or *MAGNI-* is represented by disjoined *M*, written in first position (for vowel *a*)

magnanimous,   magnetise,   magnificent,   magnitude.

Reading and writing practice — 1

1

2

3

4

5

5 *SELF*- is represented by a disjoined *S* circle written in second place. *SELF-CON* is represented by a disjoined *S* circle written in the position of the *CON*- dot. All these outlines are written in the second position (for vowel *e* in *self*)

self-defence,   self-interest,   self-evident,   self-contained,   self-service.

6 To promote speed, *TRANS*- may be shortened in most words by leaving out *N*. *TRAS* is written in first position (for vowel *a*)

transfer,   transport,   translate,   transcribe,   transmission.

7 *IN-* before *ST-R*, *SK-R* and upward *H* is represented by a small hook written in the same direction as the circle. The outlines are written in third position (for vowel *i*)

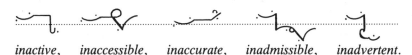

instructed, instrument, inherit, inhabit.

8 Negative words: When the prefix *IN-* means *NOT*, it is always written with stroke *N*

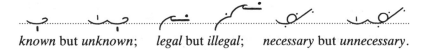

inactive, inaccessible, inaccurate, inadmissible, inadvertent.

but other negative words are distinguished from the positive by repeating the first consonant

known but *unknown*; *legal* but *illegal*; *necessary* but *unnecessary*.

Reading and writing practice — 2

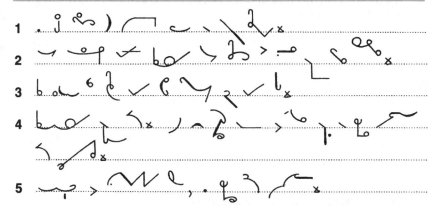

1

2

3

4

5

Suffixes and word-endings

1 The suffix *-ING* is represented by a light dot:
   a Where it would be difficult to write stroke *NG* at the end of a word

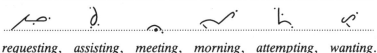

requesting, assisting, meeting, morning, attempting, wanting.

b After downward *R*
c After light straight simple downstrokes
d After most short forms (where stroke *NG* would not join easily, or a distinguishing outline is required, as with *giving*)

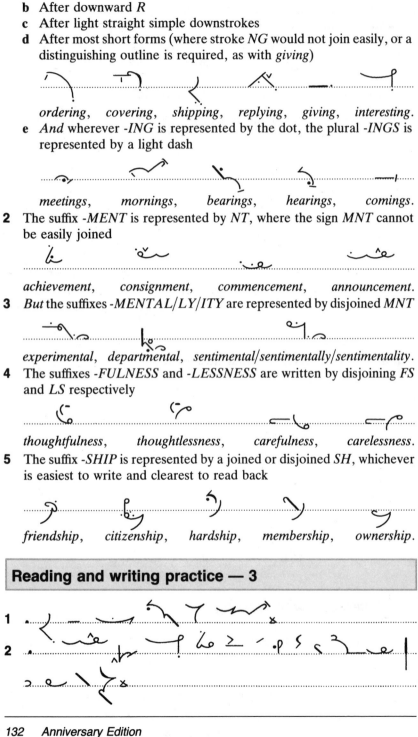

ordering, covering, shipping, replying, giving, interesting.
e *And* wherever *-ING* is represented by the dot, the plural *-INGS* is represented by a light dash

meetings, mornings, bearings, hearings, comings.
2 The suffix *-MENT* is represented by *NT*, where the sign *MNT* cannot be easily joined

achievement, consignment, commencement, announcement.
3 *But* the suffixes *-MENTAL/LY/ITY* are represented by disjoined *MNT*

experimental, departmental, sentimental/sentimentally/sentimentality.
4 The suffixes *-FULNESS* and *-LESSNESS* are written by disjoining *FS* and *LS* respectively

thoughtfulness, thoughtlessness, carefulness, carelessness.
5 The suffix *-SHIP* is represented by a joined or disjoined *SH*, whichever is easiest to write and clearest to read back

friendship, citizenship, hardship, membership, ownership.

Reading and writing practice — 3

1

2

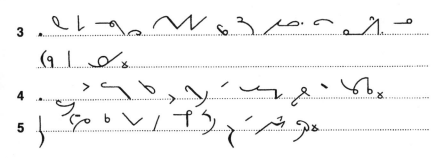

6 The suffixes *-LITY* or *-RITY*, preceded by any vowel, are represented by disjoining the preceding stroke

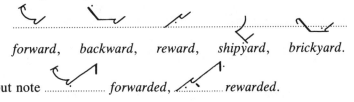

possi-b-ility, lia-b-ility, for-m-ality, simi-l-arity, ma-j-ority, mi-n-ority.

7 The word endings *-LOGICAL/LOGICALLY* are represented by disjoined *J*

chronological-ly, biological-ly, psychological-ly, physiological-ly.

8 The suffixes *-WARD* and *-YARD* are represented by half-length *W* and *Y* respectively

forward, backward, reward, shipyard, brickyard.

but note .... *forwarded,* .... *rewarded.*

9 The ending *-LY* is represented by
a stroke *L*, which can be disjoined where necessary
b *L* hook

easily, fairly, instantly, particularly, cheaply, actively.

Note: Special use of disjoining:

promptness, indebtedness, outfit.

Reading and writing practice — 4

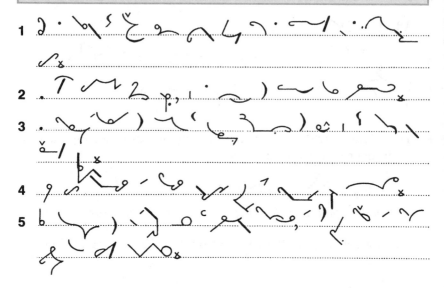

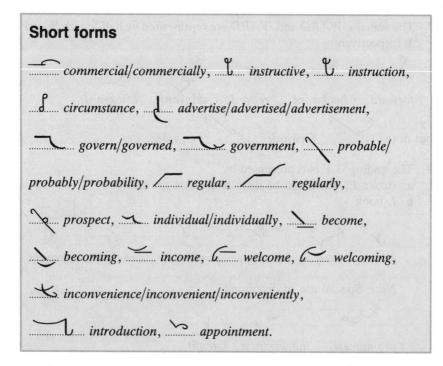

Phrases

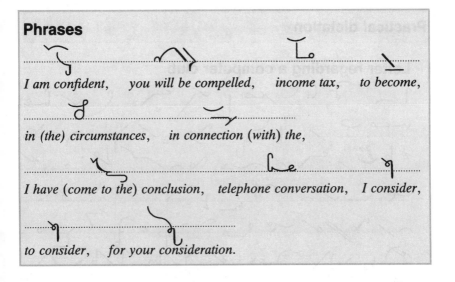

I am confident, *you will be compelled,* *income tax,* *to become,*

in (the) circumstances, *in connection (with) the,*

I have (come to the) conclusion, *telephone conversation,* *I consider,*

to consider, *for your consideration.*

Short form and phrasing practice

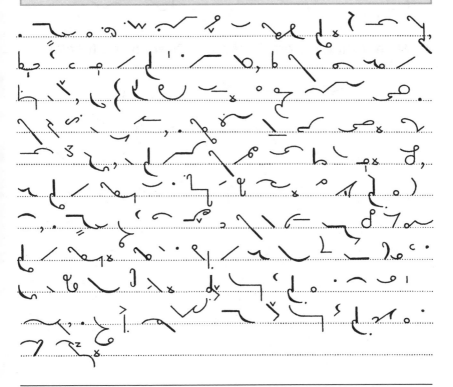

Practical dictation

1 Letter regarding a computer club

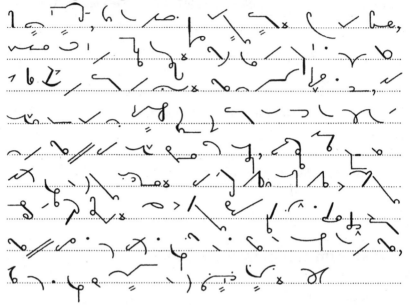

2 Memorandum from Marketing Director to all sales staff

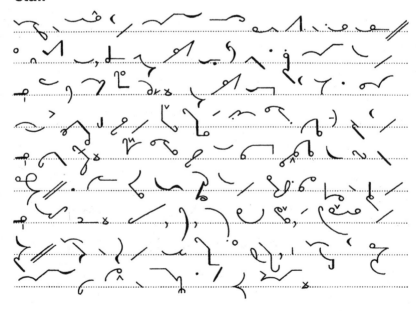

3 Memorandum from Personnel Manager to Training Manager

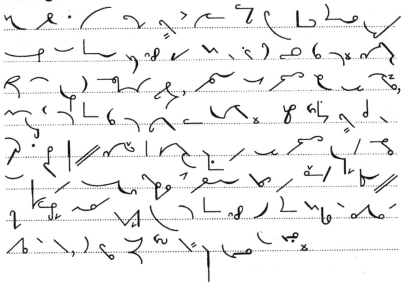

Write the following in shorthand:

1 community
2 uncommon
3 transportation
4 illegible
5 running

6 desirability
7 self-satisfied
8 connected
9 accommodate
10 inhospitable

Appendix I

Figures

Figures 0–9, except 0 and 8, are best written in shorthand

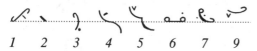

| 1 | 2 | 3 | 4 | 5 | 6 | 7 | 9 |

Other numbers, except round numbers, are represented by the ordinary arabic numerals. Round numbers are represented as follows

.....⌣..... for *hundred* or *hundredth*: ...7... *700*, ...2... *£200*.

....(.... or ...6.... for *thousand*: .5(.. *5000*, 2⌡ *£2000*, ..3.. *300 000*,

4..5... *£4500*.

....⌢.... *for million*: ..4... *4 000 000*, ..2.. *200 000 000*, ..2⌢ *£2 million*.

.....\.... for *billion*; 2\⌒ *two billions*.

....|.... *for dollar*; 2\ *two billion dollars*.

Figures combined with fractions

½ — a dash *above* the figure to which the half belongs

ī.........2̄........3̄\.......

1½   2½   3½%

¼ — a dash with an initial tick *above* the figure

ᴸ3̄........ᴸ4̄........

3¼   4¼%

¾ — a dash with a final tick

7̄¯   8̄\.......

7¾   8¾%

Dates are written

1 ⌡   ρ ⟍   ⌒⁄   22 ⌁   ⌐(⩔

1 January,   1st February,   2nd March,   22nd July,   7th April,

⌐⌡   23⌐⌒   21)⌡

3rd June,   23rd May,   21st June.

Times are written

5⌐   17 9   0930 9   7 ⌁   6 ⌁

5 o'clock,   1700 hours,   0930 hours,   7 am,   6 pm.

Appendix II

Verbatim reporting

1 When initials are dictated, they should be written as such in lower case longhand; however, in some cases a shorthand outline may be used.

	words	*initials*	
BBC		*bbc*	British Broadcasting Corporation
EC		*ec*	European Community
NASA		*nasa*	National Aeronautics and Space Administration
NATO		*nato*	North Atlantic Treaty Organisation
PIN		*pin*	Personal Identification Number
UNESCO		*unesco*	United Nations Educational, Scientific and Cultural Organisation
VAT		*vat*	Value Added Tax
VDU		*vdu*	Visual Display Unit

2 If it is necessary to indicate in your shorthand notes that a longhand abbreviation is to be used, write a fully vocalised outline for the abbreviation:

hadn't, *don't*, *isn't*, *can't*, *doesn't*, *won't*, *that's*, *it's*, *I'm*, *I'll*.

Appendix III

Short Forms

List one

The number in brackets indicates the unit in which the word is introduced.

A

a (4)

accord-ing (12)

acknowledge (19)

advantage (16)

advertise -ment-d (20)

all (4)

altogether (14)

an (4)

and (4)

any (5)

anything (5)

appointment (20)

are (7)

as (4)

B

balance (15)

balanced (15)

be (1)

because (6)

become (20)

becoming (20)

been (13)

behalf (16)

belief (15)

believe-d (15)

beyond (8)

build-ing (15)

but (1)

C

call (15)

called (15)

can (5)

cannot (13)

care (12)

cared (12)

certificate (11)

chair (12)

chaired (12)

character (19)

circumstance (20)

cold (15)

come (3)

commercial- -ly (20)

could (11)

D

danger (16)

dear (12)

deliver-y-ed (15)

description (12)

different-ce (5)

difficult (16)

difficulty (16)

distinguish- -ed (15)

do (1)

doctor, Dr (12)

during (12)

E

efficient-ly-cy (17)

equal-ly (15)

equalled (15)

especial-ly (6)	his (1)	**J**
everything (19)	hour (7)	January (3)
exchange-d (14)	how (8)	**K**
expect-ed (14)	however (12)	knowledge (19)
expenditure (13)		**L**
expensive (13)	**I**	language (4)
eye (8)	I (8)	large (4)
	immediate (11)	largely (15)
F	important-ce (18)	larger (12)
familiar-ity (14)	impossible (18)	largest (10)
February (2)	improve-d-ment (18)	liberty (12)
financial-ly (16)	in (5)	**M**
first (10)	income (20)	manufacture-d (9)
for (4)	inconvenience-t-ly (20)	manufacturer (9)
from (12)	individual-ly (20)	me (8)
	influence (10)	member (12)
G	influenced (10)	mere (12)
general-ly (13)	inform-ed (3)	more (12)
give-n (3)	information (17)	mortgage-d (16)
go (5)	inspect-ed-ion (14)	most (10)
govern-ed (20)	instruction (20)	Mr (12)
government (20)	instructive (20)	much (6)
great (17)	insurance (14)	myself (10)
guard (17)	interest (19)	**N**
	introduction (20)	near (12)
H	investigation (17)	neglect-ed (16)
had (4)	is (1)	never (3)
hand (11)	it (1)	nevertheless (15)
has (4)	itself (10)	next (10)
have (2)		nor (12)
he (9)		northern (13)
him (3)		
himself (10)		

nothing (5)		prospect (20)		special-ly (6)	
November (3)		public (17)		subject-ed (6)	
number-ed (12)		publish-ed (17)		sufficient- -ly-cy (17)	
		put (5)		sure (12)	

O

object-ed (1)		**Q**		surprise (12)	
objection (17)		quite (11)		surprised (12)	
of (4)					
on (4)		**R**		**T**	
opinion (13)		rather (19)		telegram (15)	
opportunity (18)		regular (20)		tell (15)	
organisation (17)		regularly (20)		thank-ed (7)	
organise-d (13)		remarkable (15)		that (11)	
ought (5)		remark-ed (12)		the (1)	
our (7)		remember- -ed (12)		their (12)	
ourselves (10)		represent- -ed (16)		them (2)	
over (12)		representative (16)		themselves (10)	
owe (5)		respect-ed (14)		there (12)	
owing (4)		respectful- -ly (16)		therefore (19)	
own (13)		responsible- -ility (17)		thing (3)	
owner (13)				think (2)	
		S		third (16)	
P		satisfaction (17)		this (6)	
particular (18)		satisfactory (7)		those (6)	
people (15)		sent (11)		though (10)	
pleasure (12)		several (6)		thus (6)	
practic(s)e-d (14)		shall (2)		to (1)	
principal-ly (12)		short (12)		to be (5)	
principle (12)		should (7)		together (14)	
probable- -ly-ility (20)		something (6)		told (16)	
production (17)		southern (13)		too (1)	
productive (17)		speak (6)		toward (16)	
project-ed (12)				trade (16)	

tried (16)		we (3)		within (13)	
truth (12)		welcome (20)		without (11)	
two (1)		welcoming (20)		wonderful-ly (19)	
		what (7)		word (11)	
U		when (8)		would (9)	
under (11)		whether (14)		writer (19)	
university (14)		which (1)			
usual-ly (2)		who (1)		**Y**	
		whose (9)		year (7)	
V		why (8)		yesterday (6)	
very (12)		wish (5)		you (8)	
		wished (11)		young (5)	
W		with (4)		your (7)	
was (2)					

Short forms

List two

The following short forms are not used in the book. They represent words which are less frequently used but which will be found useful in high-speed writing.

A

administrator

amalgamate

amalgamation

arbitrary

arbitrate

arbitration

arbitrator

architect-ure-al

assignment

attainment

B

bankruptcy

C

capable

characteristic

cheer

cheered

child

contentment

contingency

D

dangerous

defective

deficient-ly-cy

demonstrate

demonstration

destruction

destructive

destructively

discharge-d

E

electric

electrical

electricity

emergency

England

English

enlarge

enlargement

entertainment

enthusiastic-m

establish-ed-ment

executive

executor

expediency

F

familiarise

G

generalisation

gentleman

gentlemen

gold

I

identical

identification

imperfect-ion-ly

inconsiderate

intelligible-ly

incorporated

independent-ly-ce

indispensable-ly

influential-ly

inscribe-d

inscription

intelligence

intelligent-ly

investment

irrecoverable-ly

irregular

irrespective

irrespectively

irresponsible-ility

J

jurisdiction

justification

L

legislative

legislature

Lord

M

manuscript

mathematics

maximum

mechanical-ly

messenger

metropolitan

minimum

ministry

misfortune

monstrous

N

negligence

New York

notwithstanding

O

objectionable

objective

obstruction

obstructive

oneself

organiser

P

passenger

peculiar-ity

perform-ed

performance

perspective

practicable

prejudice-d-ial-ly

preliminary

proficient-ly-cy

proportion-ed

prospective

prospectus

publication

publisher

Q

questionable-ly

R

recoverable

reform-ed

relinquish-ed

removable

representation

reproduction

republic

republican

respective

respectively

retrospect

retrospective

S

school

schooled

selfish-ness

sensible-ly-ility

significance

significant

signify-ied

spirit

stranger

stringency

subjective

subscribe-d

subscription

substantial-ly

suspect-ed

sympathetic

T

telegraphic

thankful

U

unanimous-ly/
unanimity

uniform-ity-ly

United Kingdom

United States

United States of
America

universal

universe

V

valuation

W

whatever

whenever

Y

yard

Appendix IV

Intersections

Note: Where intersection is not practicable, write one stroke close to another as illustrated. The unit in which the intersection appears is given in brackets.

B	represents *bank* (5)		bank rate
BS	represents *business* (6)		business conference
CH	represents *charge* (8)		this charge
			free of charge
D	represents *department* (3)		foreign department
F	represents *form* (6)		necessary form
G	represents *government* (6)		government official
G	(with *N* hook) represents *beginning* (14)		at the beginning
K	represents *company* (3)		this company
Kr	represents *corporation* (18)		public corporation
L	represents *limited* in firm's name only (*KL* represents *company limited*) (3)		Robinson Limited
M	represents *manager*,		general manager
	market or		money market
	morning (10)		Monday morning
N	represents *national* or		national affairs
	enquire/enquiry/inquire/inquiry (11)		your enquiry
P	represents *party* or		Conservative Party
	policy (5)		government policy
PLS	represents *plc* (18)		Systems plc

R	represents *arrange-d-ment* (7)		make arrangements
			we have arranged
RAY	represents *require-d-ment* (7)		you may require
			will be required
			your requirement
S	represents *society* (9)		agricultural society
T	represents *attention* (8)		early attention
TH	represents *authority* or		Local Authority
	month (10)		for a month
			next month

Key to Theory Check

Unit 1

1   6

2   7

3   8

4   9

5   10

Unit 2

1   6

2   7

3   8

4   9

5   10

Unit 3

1   6

2   7

3   8

4   9

5   10

Unit 4

1   6

2   7

3   8

4   9

5   10

Unit 5

1   6

2   7

3   8

4   9

5   10

Unit 6

1   6

2   7

3   8

4   9

5   10

Unit 7

1
2
3
4
5

6
7
8
9
10

Unit 8

1
2
3
4
5

6
7
8
9
10

Unit 9

1
2
3
4
5

6
7
8
9
10

Unit 10

1
2

3
4

5
6
7

8
9
10

Unit 11

1
2
3
4
5

6
7
8
9
10

Unit 12

1
2
3
4
5

6
7
8
9
10

Unit 13

1
2
3
4
5

6
7
8
9
10

Unit 14

1
6
2
7
3
8
4
9
5
10

Unit 15

1
6
2
7
3
8
4
9
5
10

Unit 16

1
6
2
7
3
8
4
9
5
10

Unit 17

1
3
2
4

5
6
7

Unit 18

1
6
2
7
3
8
4
9
5
10

Unit 19

1
6
2
7
3
8
4
9
5
10

Unit 20

1
6
2
7
3
8
4
9
5
10

Pitman — skills that work

Shorthand skills are just one important part of the many competencies that allow entry into the world of office technology.

For further details contact:
Addison Wesley Longman Limited
Marketing Department
Edinburgh Gate
Harlow
Essex CM20 2JE

Telephone 01279 623437